THE SECOND CHILD

A Story of Hope, Abuse, Generational
Mental Illness and Addiction, and Families

Regina Toffolo

Barletta&Bellami

*To: Alexander
With much
appreciation,
Regina Toffolo*

To Randi, who, when she was alive, always liked to say that when she first met me, she thought I was crazy, but then she realized I was only being honest.

CONTENTS

	2
Title Page	2
Dedication	4
Preface	8
Chapter 1	11
Chapter 2	38
Chapter 3	48
Chapter 4	62
Chapter 5	69
Chapter 6	75
Chapter 7	84
Chapter 8	90
Chapter 9	104
Chapter 10	118
Chapter 11	136
Chapter 12	146
Chapter 13	159
Chapter 14	167
Chapter 15	180
Chapter 16	190
Epilogue	199

Acknowledgement 206

PREFACE

It has been a great pleasure for me to write this book, and I hope others find it worthwhile. Writing the book has taken me to highs and sometimes to lows, but it may not be for the reasons you would expect. Many people have read this book and remarked how brave the book is, and how writing it must have been cathartic for me.

I have to say that absolutely nothing about writing the book was due to bravery. I'm basically a coward at heart. The idea of the book came to me one day when I was indulging in my usual bad habit of comparing myself to other people unfavorably. On that particular day, it was my high school friends. They are wonderful people and it was a privilege to be part of their circle in those days, but their lives now are very different from mine. Not that they judge me - they don't - but the fact remains: they have had the life it seemed we were promised in high school, and my life has been something different.

So on this particular day, I felt an overwhelming urge to yell to the world, and to them, and to the Universe, "This is why! This is why my life didn't turn out like yours!" There was no bravery involved. It was a relief to finally say, "This is my world and the history I wake up with every day. This is why."

Nor was the primary outcome of writing the book some kind of catharsis. None of the stories here are new. I've dealt with them in therapy, and they have been known to quite a few for quite some time. I would say this book has been more transformative. Throughout the process of writing it, I learned things about myself, I saw myself a different way. Old photos of me in my nerd phase that used to make me cringe stopped making me cringe and instead made me happy. At least one photo, of my brother, Tony, started making me cringe, which probably should have happened a long time ago.

The second transformation I experienced is around the way I look at my children. Before, all I could see was their struggles and the impact that has had on them and on me. Now I can see positives where I did not see them before, like the fact that they are at heart loving, caring people. It sounds silly, but they are boys that love their stray cats. That's what a mother hopes for in her children above all else, the capacity for basic human kindness.

The final transformation I experienced while writing this book regards the anger I felt at some of the people in the book. Somehow writing the book took the anger away. Writing their parts of the story reminded me they have reasons, too, just like me. Out of that realization came forgiveness.

Ultimately though, while I have gotten the relief I sought, and while I have experienced a transformation, there was a more important reason for writing the book, and for continuing on when I got discouraged. When one of my friends asked me why I was writing the book, this is what immediately came to mind:

If this book helps one person with a narcissistic parent, one person who is a victim of incest, one person with an alcohol problem, one person with a man problem, one person with children with mental health issues, writing the book is worth it. Even if it's only one person.

There were times when I was writing this book when I wanted to throw in the towel. Why would anyone care, why should anyone care? Lots of people have stories, there's nothing particularly interesting about mine. I would lie on the couch and close my eyes then in a sort of despair, ready to give up. But then a voice would come to me, "Keep writing. The book has a higher purpose." The message from the Universe was very clear.

I have no idea how any 'higher purpose' will come to fruition, or if I will even know if it does. I will likely never know if the book has helped someone. Few of us ever see where the ripples we start end up. I just have to start the ripple and let God do what He wills with it. Which is apropos, as that is my entire life.

Enjoy.

CHAPTER 1

How It Began

Once upon a time, there was a pretty little girl. She was a bright, funny, whimsical, idealistic, and caring little girl, who yes, quite frankly, could be a little bratty, but one who had an inherent innocence. She was The Second Child.

I don't say that because my older (adopted) brother didn't matter, he desperately did. I say that because as the second biological child, I was expected to be the real deal, to be a textbook carbon copy of the perfection that was my oldest sibling, my sister Betsy, and he wasn't, at least not in the same way.

* * *

When I was a child, I wanted to go live in a tree. There was a tree by a construction site that I wasn't supposed to go to that was perfect for climbing. It seemed to have countless wide, leafy-green boughs. In my mind, I could see a Swiss Family Robinson tree house nestled in its branches. The tree was a safe place where for me, the rest of the world, and my family, faded away. My plan was to put my Catholic school uniform and other clothes in a grocery store paper bag, take a house key, and live in that tree. I would go to school in the day, and sneak into the house for food at night. But I loved my family.

We all have secrets in a family, and things we do not say. The tragedies that shape our lives that live beneath the sea of people, and things, and events. You can't readily see those tragedies, but they live there just the same, secretly shaping our loves and our lives into a path other people seem to recognize, not understanding the reasons why. My life was shaped by my secrets, and by my mother. Because my sister wasn't the problem, the problem was the way my mother saw us.

My achingly beautiful, and terrible, and delicate, fragile mother. My mother wasn't fragile in a physical sense by any means. She was quite tall and carried herself with regal bearing. Proper posture was always a must. Mom always dressed very formally, as was expected in those times, wearing conservative but colorful and stylish dresses. She wore dresses, of course, pants for women were out of the question when I was growing up. Her short dark brown hair was always glamorously curled, and her luminous big eyes and high cheekbones gave her a classic beauty like Greta Garbo, my father's favorite actress.

No, my mother's delicacy and fragility were emotional although I did not really understand that as a child. I only always saw her frowning disapproval of me. Even when I was young though, I did know that while my mother was demanding at home, outside of the house her tone was rather meek and shy, a direct contrast to the mother I saw at home. When she was at home, my mother always smelled vaguely of vitamins. When we went out, my mother smelled like flowery perfume.

I'll never know what secrets shaped my mother. Whatever they were, they went with her to her grave. My father's secrets were somewhat revealed, but in the end, they weren't important other than the fact that they must have been the reason why he married my mother. Maybe my parents should never have been parents, at least my mother should probably not have been. And to think they gave my mother not one, but two adopted children, one when she was almost forty-five. But she loved me before she died, and that is all that ever really mattered.

* * *

From the time I was a small child, there were battle lines in my house. Fault lines between the team that was my mother and

The Firstborn Child, my sister, Betsy, and the team that was my father and the rest of us, my older adopted brother, Tony, my younger adopted brother, Chris, and myself. There were other fault lines, like the one between my mother and me. Fault lines between my older brother and me. Fault lines between my younger brother and me.

For all I somehow knew this, I still defended my family vehemently that time I was in a psych ward when I was eighteen. Why do we do that? Then the shrink told my father there was nothing wrong with me despite me being in the throes of alcoholism, and major depression, and what was much later to be recognized as Bipolar II disorder. But that was 1977, before most people could see that in an 18-year-old privileged white girl. Certainly before they had effective medications to treat it.

I'm an old lady now, and one might think this would all be buried history. But being old, one finds oneself looking at the entirety of one's life and taking a reckoning. Either this can lead to old-age despair, or it can lead to an unburdening. I hope mine is the latter, as somehow, even to this day, I have still reckoned with not being my sister. I have raised sons who, though they are wonderful, smart, loving people, have faced grave challenges. Hence, in some eyes, my sons may not appear to live up to my sister's standards, the arbitrary standards of the socio-economic-intellectual class from whence I came. The standards my sister's children seem to exceed, a PhD, an MD, and a CPA between them.

To a large degree, although not entirely, the differences between my family and my sister's family are undoubtedly rooted in my own childhood. The powerful and destructive consequences of the family fault lines present in my childhood have spanned across lifetimes and across generations.

***

"Raayyyy-geena," my mother would call in her sing-song voice. That never boded well. I'd be hiding, reading, escaping, watching TV, and there would be something that wasn't done, or something that wasn't done well enough. Most likely, it was something like the heat registers in my room not passing inspection when I cleaned my room. Or my mother would clomp up from her many forays into 'the basement,' and you knew you suddenly needed to look busy or there'd be hell to pay.

My family and I lived in a split-level house in Maryland, just outside Washington, DC. It wasn't a big house by today's McMansion standards, but it was certainly large enough for the six of us. I lived in that house all my growing years, and it was a beautiful house, and I remember it with the sweet wistfulness that comes with age. There were five levels in our house, each with their own unique purpose. The top floor of the house had all the bedrooms, then there were a living room level, a street level with the kitchen, a lower living room, and the infamous basement.

On the top floor, my bedroom was pink with hardwood floors and oversized windows that brightened the room and let lots of fresh air in. It was large, almost as large as my parents'. I had shared this room with Tony when we were little, but then my parents moved him into one of the smaller rooms he later shared with my younger brother. Not sure why I got the big bedroom and my brothers got the little room, but then, my brothers, being adopted, were different. We always knew there were differences in the way we were treated. Betsy's room was slightly smaller than mine, and had a built-in desk that was one of my favorite hiding places when we played hide and seek.

The living room level was my favorite room in the house. It had a golden carpet and luxurious, blue-green floor-length brocade drapes embroidered in gold to match the carpet. The dominant feature in the living room was the smooth-varnished baby grand piano. One might say the piano was the most important piece of furniture in the house. My mother always said a house wasn't a house without a piano. It was a point of pride when company came and we got to put the baby grand top up.

On the street level were the kitchen and dinette with their matching gold-flecked white counters with a gleaming glass china cabinet hanging from above over the kitchen island. My mother cooked all the time, at least when she wasn't sewing, and the kitchen always smelled of paprika and cinnamon. Every day, at least until my mother went to work when I was twelve, we had family dinner in that dinette promptly at 5 p.m., my father dominating the conversation as he expounded on a myriad of topics, told corny Dad jokes, and then whipped my ice cream into delicious softness.

The TV was in the lower living room. Here also could be found the sewing machine and an ironing board. These had to live here, heaven forbid if you watched TV without working.

Then came the notorious basement. I liked the coolness of the basement, but it was dark with brown flooring. It did not have the benefit of the large windows we had elsewhere in the house and so smelled strongly of mothballs and wood shavings. One part of the basement included my father's workbench, the other parts were storage. One room was general storage, and then there was one room with many intricate shelves where my mother kept her things. In the back corner, there was the little converted bathroom that was my doll room. Not that I had dolls I wanted. Maybe one could say I was ungrateful. I had what were probably antique valuable dolls with a whole rack of handmade clothes of silk and other things. But it was 1965, and I wanted a Barbie.

My mother and the basement always meant a particular kind of dread. There was always dread, but there were degrees. Later on in life, I realized my mother was so invested in that basement because she lived through the Great Depression. Today, psychologists would call her behavior 'hoarding,' My mother needed the reassurance of having things. Things stored and saved. Things so she wouldn't run out of things. Things moved here and there and back again, so she could still be sure she had things. These weren't necessarily important things. They might include costume jewelry or little bathroom soaps, but whatever they were, these things were important to my mother. Those were the things in her little room with shelves. The rest of the basement could get very disorganized with a whole bunch of evidently less important things, but still things just the same. That was what we were expected to clean up. I can't say when chores like this started, but probably somewhere around age five. That's when my piano lessons started anyway. I just tried to find someplace else to be. The best place was at the house of the family across the street where life was fun, and the mother curled the daughter's hair and served corn on the cob with the little corn cob holders, and they had a 64-color crayon box, and we watched *Cinderella* on a color TV.

* * *

Betsy was the firstborn of the four children in my family but she was not really part of the rest of us. She was seven years older than my older brother, Tony, eleven years older than I, and fourteen years older than my younger brother, Chris. I guess it's understandable why Betsy overshadowed us. When I was seven, Betsy was eighteen. I was little, and she was big. One of us was a grown-up and one of us was a child. She was more like an aunt than a sister.

As a child, I looked up to my sister in awe, even a sort of worship. Her life seemed so exciting and romantic. While she was in the right age group, Betsy never got involved in the turmoil of the 60s, it wouldn't suit her image. For Betsy, life still seemed to unfold like the happy 50s. Often Betsy would take me places like trips to her college campus to see her sorority house. Or I would eagerly watch her as she combed her ebony hair into soft waves and picked the perfect lipstick for a date. Vicariously experiencing aspects of Betsy's life was mesmerizing to me.

My sister and mother were always devoted to each other. It was a devotion that excluded the rest of us, even my father. Betsy never saw my mother the way the rest of us did, probably because she was never on the other end of it. Together, my mother and sister shared every grand plan, every confidence, every trouble, anything a girl would want to talk about. That sharing was between my mother and sister, it was a sole investment.

Despite the dynamic with my mother, I didn't aspire to be my sister, nor I was ever consumed with jealousy. Our perspectives of our mother and father were so different, and even then, I instinctively knew mine was truer. Also, I was more introspective than Betsy and my inner life was a comfort to me. Even as a child, I had to become introspective, outside sources were too unreliable for me. So my feelings were more complicated than jealousy. I only felt like I was never good enough compared to Betsy, and I placed the blame for that on myself.

The way my mother saw us was not Betsy's fault, and Betsy never lorded it over me, nor did she inflict any judgment on the rest of us for siding with mand y father in family fights. Overall, Betsy was mostly a benevolent, though somewhat distant 'aunt-ish' influence across our emotional divide, except the one time in Ninth Grade when she smashed my *Jesus Christ Superstar* albums on the bathroom floor because I wouldn't stop playing them.

My older brother, Tony, was short and dark-haired with an oval face. He was my first love. I suppose in some ways that's rather Freudian, but I did need him, and I absolutely idolized him. I can't say that there was a specific reason. In our pre-school years, Tony was the one closest to me. He took care of me, he protected me, he amused me. Even my mother always said he doted on me and was very protective of me when I was a baby. In my early and grade school years, there only seemed to be the two of us, Tony and I. Betsy was way ahead of us, Chris was far enough behind to have a different life.

About the time Tony started grade school, our relationship changed, but even after Tony started school, whatever Tony did, I wanted to be there with him. Tony would go on adventures in the woods with his friends to build forts, and I would insist that I be included though he hated that. I was his tag-along little sister, but that didn't daunt me. In general, when Tony wasn't paying me attention, I would live up to my bratty reputation and pester him incessantly. After all, bad attention was better than no attention at all.

At times after we got a little older, Tony would include me in his activities for whatever inexplicable reason - probably boredom. When Tony was in middle school and I was still in grade school, I remember sitting in his room where he played Jethro Tull and Cheech and Chong records. He especially liked the Cheech and Chong song about Sister Mary Elephant. "Class, Class, Class, SHUT UP!" I guess Tony liked that because he didn't seem to get along too well with the nuns at our school. Tony would play that song, and we would laugh, and I would feel fortunate in the moment.

I would feel complete.

I have very few memories of Chris when we were young. He was blond and husky even as a child. His blond hair definitely marked him as different in our family. I never needed him like I did Tony, nor was I in awe of him like I was of Betsy. When we were little, I took no small satisfaction from bossing Chris around, which probably did not endear me to him. Later in life - almost all of my life - Chris didn't like me. By the time I was in middle school, Chris became superior. For one thing, by middle school I was already getting into trouble, and Chris didn't like my attitude. Maybe I deserved this, maybe it was payback, I don't know. Maybe I hadn't earned the right to be hurt by this, but I was. It hurt that he didn't like me.

* * *

For whatever reason, Betsy was often out of the house when we were little. She traveled quite a way by bus to go to a posh Catholic school in NW DC where my aunt was a drama teacher. A lot of hours on the bus, a lot of hours at school, a lot of hours at ballet lessons. She mostly just flitted in, a simple tease about what perfection was (that we weren't), and then she would be away again. Except I remember her on occasion in battles in the family war.

We had rituals in my house. Every Sunday, we would go to church. Every Sunday, my Aunt Bobby, my mother's sister, would come to dinner and give me my piano lesson, and every Sunday my mother and father would have a screaming match. Not that there weren't screaming matches any other day of the week, because there were.

As with most people, the fights were always about the same things. One was money. One was the kids. My father was doing his best to protect us, the three younger children, from my mother, and surely, we needed protection. My mother was the household tyrant. But my sister was always on my mother's side. I remember my sister once daringly faced off with my father defending my mother's point of view. Later in her life, when she was forty-five, my sister finally realized that my mother was crazy. She then said she had always wondered in those days why my mother's family didn't step in to help my mother deal with my father and his anger. At forty-five, my sister finally realized it was because my mother's family knew my father was not to blame.

Frequently, my parents' yelling matches devolved into discussions of divorce, which was its own trauma in a Catholic family in 1965. My father would take the three younger kids away with him, that's where we wanted to be, right? And we did. It felt good to have my father defend us even though I sometimes felt guilty about it. Somehow though, I also knew deep inside that I would miss my mother terribly.

What we really needed was a mother who loved us, and a divorce, taking us away, couldn't fix that, nor could anyone around us. In later years, when my neighbor Mrs. A. was at my younger brother's wedding, she proceeded to tell my husband all the terrible things that had happened to me growing up. To this day, I don't know exactly what she told my husband (now ex and deceased), but it was a lot. I'm sure it included the dread that always came when I was at Mrs. A.'s house and the phone would ring. We all knew it would be my mother wanting me to come home. There was always something I was supposed to be doing.

But the neighbors couldn't fix things either, could they? Things apparently everyone could see.

It wasn't all bad. Sometimes my mother would be mad at me, and I would make her laugh, and when she couldn't help it, she would giggle, then everything would be okay. It didn't hurt me to learn to sew and play piano and clean, and to learn how to work hard, and how to do things well. My children didn't get that, unfortunately. But they got other things that I was able to give, little bits in the tsunami that was their lives. At least, I think most of the time, they knew I loved them.

* * *

To hear tell, my mother had an idyllic childhood other than the Great Depression. She had parents who were devoted to each other and devoted to their children. Siblings devoted to each other. There was a failed business in the midst of the Depression and the Great Dustbowl, but my grandparents triumphed over that and sent all their children, including the girls, to college, and this was back in the late 30's. My aunt was a triple-major and she considered becoming a professional pianist. My mother, despite what she later expected of us academically, was not a great student, something I only found out later in life. But she did get a degree, in Home Economics, the perfect preparation for being the perfect wife.

I have no idea what happened to my mother but something must have. My Aunt Bobby was a great storyteller. I guess it was her background in Drama, one of her college majors. My aunt was tall - taller than my mother - and large-boned as befitted her German-Swiss ancestry. She had none of that movie star beauty my mother had - that came from the Irish side of the family - but my aunt was a handsome woman. She never married, a great flaw in my mother's mind, but apparently, my aunt's only prospect for marriage had been killed in World War II.

My aunt was always very supportive of me as I was growing up, unlike my mother, but she could also be very intimidating, for example. after finding out I hadn't practiced for my piano lesson. Still, she was a great gift in my life, and I always loved learning about family history from her.

My whole childhood I heard about my mother's perfect family, but my aunt also once told a story about how my grandfather's grain store, the family business, burned down while my grandfather was away on a trip. Aunt Bobby said they all stood in the yard: my grandmother, my mother, my aunt and uncles, all holding hands, and helplessly watched while the silo completely burned down. My mother didn't remember this. This event isn't enough, all on its own, to explain my mother's many idiosyncrasies, but you begin to see the dichotomy between the fabled perfect life and the reality.

***

I came into the world late in my parent's life. My sister was born when my parents were thirty. After seven years of trying for another baby, they adopted my brother. I wasn't born until my mother was almost forty-one. My parents tried and tried to have me. Well, not me exactly, but another perfect baby like Betsy. There were miscarriages and infertility. I could never envision this series of events, not because I couldn't envision them having sex, but because of the war my parents started fighting when I was very young. Although sex was an issue, too, as my mother was totally anti-sex. It was one of The Rules.

And there were rules. Rules upon rules. The main rule was around being Catholic. We went to Catholic schools, we had Catholic friends, we did Catholic things. We were defined by being Catholic; it was a fundamental part of our family identity.

The second rule was of paramount importance. We all had to get married. That was our ultimate goal and purpose in life. Everything in my house was about getting married. When my younger brother was a little overweight as a small child, my mother said the worst thing she could possibly say. She said no one would ever marry him if he had a little pot belly. He was a small child, probably age three, pudgy with baby fat. Chris did grow to be quite tall, and retained some of his childhood weight, but he did get two women to marry him, contrary to my mother's prediction.

Everything about my childhood when my sister was in college and early twenties, and when I was at a ten-year-younger impressionable age, was about her achieving that single aim. Men went parading through. Some were too short. Some were going bald. Some were the wrong religion. One sent her roses every day for a while, but she didn't like him.

But always, always, my mother and sister were talking about that. My sister even went to grad school for the sole purpose of meeting the right man, although now she denies that. (And in fairness to her, she did not do that to her own daughters.) Eventually, grad school was the ticket that worked. Heaven forbid my sister would end up single like my dear and loving aunt. That would be a disaster beyond reckoning.

The marriage rule was closely related to another rule about appearance. In my mother's eyes, a person's value was greatly dependent on how they looked. If you were a girl, you had to be pretty. If you were a boy, you had to grow to be reasonably tall, at least approaching six feet. Boy or girl, you had to be thin. My mother herself was movie-star beautiful (except for her flat chest which I unfortunately inherited), and she expected us all to follow in her footsteps.

Another rule in the house was the one about being the smartest. My mother was exceptionally vain about that. My father was a genius, and that is not an exaggeration. Certainly, we had to be the best like my father.

And those weren't all; there were other rules. One was about working. My mother herself was a workaholic to a wildly unreasonable degree. She was always sewing or cooking with never a minute's rest. My aunt once told a story about my mother going to visit her parents at their third-floor apartment building in DC that had no elevator. My mother took her sewing machine and made my father carry it up all three flights. My mother couldn't just sit and visit with someone, even her own parents.

So we children, too, always had to be working. If you were watching TV, you had to be sewing. The house needed to be cleaned perfectly. If you were at the neighbors, you had to come home. You could play piano. But always be doing something. Even if you were playing games with your father, Mom would walk by with her nose in the air and sniff disapprovingly.

The last rule, save everything, even the most insignificant thing. Never throw anything out. Hence, the basement. Also related, never spend money. I'm sure these rules were a result of the Great Depression and my mother's experience of it in her impressionable teenage years.

For a while, money became the other battle in the war, besides the kids. My father was an electrical engineer, later a nuclear physicist. We weren't poor. We weren't rich either, like my cousins on my father's side. But when I was seven, my father retired to work on his PhD. Then the money got tight. My father would spend money anyway. He would buy us nickel candy, and then say 'mum's the word' because he knew it meant a world of hurt if Mom found out. But we weren't supposed to lie, were we? That was an anti-Catholic thing. Eventually, my father went back to work, and my mother went to work, and life changed, and there was enough money. But it was still a rule that you didn't spend it.

So those were The Rules I was born into in my parents' middle-aged life. Be Catholic. Get married. Be pure and virginal until then. Always be the prettiest. Always be the smartest. Always be working. Never throw anything out. Never spend money.

In essence, my mother was always trying to completely perfect her environment, surely to compensate for some deep-rooted insecurity. My mother needed her children to be perfect, she needed her surroundings to be perfect, and she needed to feel like she would always have enough. These days, a psychiatrist would likely diagnose my mother with narcissistic personality disorder along with clinical depression and an anxiety disorder. At least, that was my experience of it, and later, this became my understanding of it.

Some of this has helped me in life, but mostly, the trouble was that the rules were just so extreme, as I was to learn.

* * *

The Rules were my mother's rules, not my father's. My father wasn't about rules. He valued knowledge and he loved to have fun. He bowled, and played chess, and played with us kids. He lived life exuberantly, at least until he died when he was sixty-four and I was twenty-three, probably in a large part due to me in my lost years of alcoholism.

Fairly recently, when I posted about my father on Facebook, one of my high school friends commented, "Your mother and father were always a study in opposites, but all my memories of your father are good ones." (In other words, your mother was a bitch.)

After my father died, I found I was always a little uncomfortable when I saw pictures of him. Then I realized it was because they never could capture him, the sheer power and force and zest of him. Also because he had that skinny face. The face I got from him, the chin I got from him that my mother hated and my older brother mocked because he knew it bothered me. But my father was at least fit and trim, a bit taller than my mother, another social must. He always made me feel safe, the familiar smell of his cherry pipe tobacco and his musky Dad-suits filling me with comfort.

While my mother was all about working, my father was all about playing games with us, and teaching us to ride bikes, and watching football, and marveling at the science of the universe, and even driving in silly circles just to amuse us. One of my favorite times was always when he took us to the playground, and he would push me on the swings, and I would fly high, higher, and higher, until I imagined I was flying, until I imagined I was free.

My father was also an exuberant Catholic. An Easter person, with great and fantastical ideas about the Heaven that awaited us which he frequently delighted in sharing with us. My mother was a forbidding Catholic. She was always worried about us getting into Heaven. There were only two things pertinent to that – go to church on Sunday, more days than that preferably, and don't have premarital sex, which became an issue in the 60s and greatly became an issue for me, given the things that were about to happen to me.

* * *

I myself was not good at rules. I was a failure at one of the biggest rules before I even started. I wasn't pretty like Betsy. My sister had that aquiline Italian beauty that was exotic and exceptional, with rich, dark hair tone and my mother's high cheekbones. I personally had that unfortunate narrow face with the long, pointy chin like my father, at least according to my mother. I always wondered why my mother married my father if she didn't like it. Certainly, she didn't like it in me. This was an Original Sin, only this one could not be baptized away.

Original Sin was a Catholic thing. Being Catholic was complicated, but I did take it to heart. I dutifully went to church on Sunday and whenever the Catholic school took us - at least until I hit puberty.

The complicated part, which was a lot, was the sinning. There were three kinds of sins as well as being non-Catholic, although strictly speaking, I don't know that you could call that a sin. All of these sins determined your end-of-life status. There were Original Sins, and Venial Sins, and Mortal Sins. The Original Sin you were born with, no good reason why, just some silly story about an Adam and Eve and an apple. Luckily, baptism took care of that. Pity the babies who died before they were baptized. They went to Limbo.

Venial Sins were things like lying and disobeying your parents, certainly in my wheelhouse. Mortal Sins were things like murder - I wasn't in danger of that. Those would send you to Hell for sure. The Venial Sins would end you up in Purgatory for who knows how long. I never could figure out how many Venial Sins could also end you up in Hell, but I was sure there was a limit. Then a Venial Sinner like me could end up in Hell, too. Sure, you could go to Confession and take care of things, but I wasn't even sure I could remember what seemed like would be a very long list of my sins.

People who committed suicide, like my grandfather, were doomed to everlasting Hell. This was for rejecting the tremendous gift of life God gave them. This never seemed fair to me, suffering on top of suffering.

Non-Catholics, even the ones who were good people, just didn't go to Heaven. Where did the good non-Catholics go?

Then there were my concerns about the marriage rule. My mother had come from a family of two boys and two girls, and one boy had gotten married and one hadn't, and one girl had gotten married, and one hadn't. From this, in my tender years, I concluded that when my sister got married, which she inevitably would, that meant I would be the sister who wouldn't. It didn't work out that way exactly, but in the end, I guess it did. One brother is married, and one brother isn't. My sister stayed married, and I didn't. But there were other reasons for that for me, an awareness that would only come later.

The smart rule wasn't a problem for me. My intelligence was the only thing my mother liked about me. She would always come home breathlessly excited after going to a parent-teacher conference where she received my standardized test scores. All through grade school and high school, I had the highest scores in my class. My mother would brag to her friends about this. At the time, I would be happy about my mother being happy, but while this succeeded in making me undeservedly vain when I was young, as I got older I realized that this obviously isn't the same as real accomplishment, nor was I as smart as I thought I would be in the wider world.

The rules that caused me the most misery when I was young were the 'house' ones, that ones that controlled our daily pattern of living. This included the ones about always working, and about saving everything and not spending money. Nothing could ever be wasted in my house, not even the smallest crumb. At age seven, I can remember sitting with a spatula endlessly trying to get that last piece of jelly out of the jar, and carefully handling the knife be sure to cut the melons close to the rind so none of the precious fruit would be wasted. We had to save every jar we ever bought until we had a cabinet full and my father would loudly opine, "Jars without tops, and tops without jars," and then we would clean the cabinet out a bit. But we needed those jars; we certainly could never throw any leftovers away.

With a rare exception like the Hot Wheels set we got for Christmas one year, toys had to be handmade, not bought. If I wanted something, my mother would say, "Isn't it nice you'll be able to have that in Heaven?" But in that era, it's probably true now also, having a Barbie was a thing. I dearly wanted a Barbie. One day, my mother and I made a rare trip to Toys-R-Us, a fabulous place. I was so happy! I don't know why we were fortunate enough to go there that day; we never went usually. While we were there, my mother actually bought me a toy. It was a Barbie knock-off, and better yet, marked down because it had been on the store display. She was called Franny. But she wasn't a Barbie, and you could tell she had been on display. When I was forty-three, and going through my second divorce, I finally bought myself a Barbie for company.

The second 'house' rule that caused misery was the one about endless chores. I did work a lot, but no matter how much I did, it was never, ever enough. Fortunately, playing piano counted, I could get out of a few things that way and I liked it. It was the sewing and the cleaning and the never-being-able-to-watch-TV-without-working that was a problem.

Early on, Tony and I had most of the upstairs housework. We would alternate, he vacuuming and dusting the living room, and I the bedrooms, and Heaven forbid you would you miss a spot. Then the next week, we would trade. Vacuuming had to be precise, either four times slowly or seven times quickly in each spot. If you missed something and it didn't pass inspection, you had to go back and do it again.

My experience with sewing was similar. If you misplaced a stitch, even in a particularly difficult piece of a garment, you had to go back, rip it out, and do it again. And again and again if need be. In adulthood, my mother always said I was good at sewing when I was young, but I never felt that way at the time.

There were slightly different rules for Tony and me. First of all, he didn't have to sew. My mother did want Tony to read books and such which he wasn't too keen on. I, on the other hand, loved to read. I would sneak and pretend to be vacuuming while really I was reading. This worked until I got caught, which I always did.

Generally speaking, whatever we wanted to do, my mother wanted us to do the opposite. Less than perfection in any of our endeavors wasn't an option. Among other things, failure could likely mean cleaning the infamous basement.

* * *

When I wrote the first draft of this chapter, my middle son, my first reader, looked at it and said, "Mom, you have to explain what 'hell to pay' meant." I replied, "Well, my mother didn't beat me." But then I remembered The Board. Much to my surprise, after thirty-five years of sobriety and fifteen years of therapy, I only just now remember that.

The Board was a 2 x 4 my mother kept above a cabinet in the hallway to the kitchen. I remember vividly being the victim of it more than once, the clearest memory being when I had visited my tree, the tree I wanted to run away to. I don't know how, but my mother always knew. The tree was near a construction site, and my mother didn't think it was safe for me. At least she had a legitimate reason for that.

After more thought, I remembered all the other times my mother used The Board, or threatened to, depending on how badly I had broken The Rules. The Board was always a lingering threat. Heaven forbid my mother should head for the cabinet. That feeling was terrifying. It felt as scary as the Wicked Witch of the West in the movie which I had watched with my neighbors on their color TV, just like I had *Cinderella*.

My brothers and I had a sneaky way of dealing with that terror. When my mother was out of the house sometimes, the three of us, Tony, Chris and I, would march around the kitchen together singing, "Oh Wee Oh. Oh Oh. Oh Wee Oh," just like the soldiers at the witch's castle near the end of the movie. Tony was the ringleader. Then we'd jubilantly sing the relieving chorus, "Ding Dong, the Witch is dead, the Wicked Witch, the Wicked Witch, the Wicked Witch is dead!" What a thing to be wishing the death of your mother. I didn't really wish she were dead. I just wished she were different.

I'm sure there were other things, I don't really remember. When I was slightly older, I vaguely recall flinching one time out of context, and so there must have been something. It had to have been my mother. My father never disciplined us.

In any event, wherever you were, whatever you were doing, in your heart of hearts you always knew…

That Mom would be coming to find you.

* * *

In some families with an abusive parent, it may be common for the children to band together to survive it. That was a rare occurrence in my family. There was only one sure way to get yourself out of being in trouble for breaking any of The Rules, and that was to distract my mother. The absolute best way to distract my mother was to get one of your siblings in worse trouble. This never included Betsy, she was perfect, but certainly it was a game that Tony, Chris and I played. We would find things out about each other, a missed duty, a visit to a place we weren't supposed to go to, skipping church on Sunday, whatever it may be. We saved up the worst things we knew about each other, and then when we were called on the carpet ourselves, we would reveal the dirt we had on another that was hopefully worse than whatever our particular infraction was. Then Mom would move on to the bigger rule-breaker and leave us alone.

Hence, the normal familial bonds between my brothers and I were forever torn, and the family fault lines between us began to form. Maybe some children would have been less selfish, but certainly in our house when it came to my mother, it was every man for himself.

* * *

Besides The Rules and their consequences, there was another thing of note that was a pervasive truth in my life growing up. Per my mother, my father was crazy. Yes, I loved my father, and yes, he defended me, and yes, he taught me, and yes, he shared his celebration of life with me. But my mother was fighting The War, and she would use any means at her disposal to win it.

My father was the son of Italian immigrants. When I heard this story when I was eighteen, I was very moved. My grandfather came to America to escape poverty in northern Italy before he married my grandmother. He was a skilled worker in tile and terrazzo looking to find his fortune. By the time my grandmother came to America, her ship had to sail in a roundabout way to avoid the mines in the ocean during World War I. It took two months. My grandmother arrived in New York, Ellis Island, on her birthday, and then went out and got married on the very same day.

My grandfather was dead before I was born, although that detail is kind of hazy, maybe it was shortly after. My knowledge of this is based on oral history, this time from my mother. She was a notoriously unreliable source of family history since she always massaged the truth to suit her needs. So either it was just before or shortly after I was born, but in any event, I never knew my grandfather. He committed suicide in the days when it meant you would go to hell if you were Catholic. I cannot remember once my father ever speaking of his father, which I didn't notice as odd until my children were born and I talked about my deceased father all the time. Later, when my sister was forty-five and went on her mission to understand why my mother was crazy, more of the story came out. Apparently, my grandfather was an alcoholic who beat his wife. He ended his days in a job that other family members gave him out of pity as a night watchman at one of my uncle's factories.

My mother talked about my grandfather a lot. She told me about how he shot himself in his basement when he was sixty-four. My father was probably forty. I spent many hours envisioning that death scene, and envisioning my grandmother finding him, not knowing then that she might have been relieved by it. But the blood, and the hole in the head, and, I suppose, brains spilled everywhere. My visions of it were gruesome, a fate worse than normal death. Why did my mother tell me, a young impressionable child, this story? I guess it was part of her narrative that my father was crazy. My grandfather obviously was, right?

Again based on my mother's unreliable history, the story goes that sometime after my grandfather killed himself, my father checked himself into a mental hospital for three months, or maybe six, depending on what version you got. According to my mother, my father was fine before that, but apparently, while he went in 'sane,' he came out 'crazy.'

To my knowledge, my father wasn't crazy. He never went to a mental ward again. He never took any medication. He wasn't an alcoholic either. He was a steady civil servant employee who rarely missed work, a researcher for the Navy for twenty-five years. He never failed in any obligation to us, to the Catholic Church, or to his many activities. He was a Steady Eddie in every way. Except for maybe his Italian temper, but even then, he never beat my mother with one exception. He hit my mother when my sister wanted to move away, but my mother didn't want to let my sister go.

Per my sister's analysis later in life, to translate my mother's diagnosis, it really meant that for the thirteen years or so that my parents had already been married when my grandfather committed suicide, my father was devoted to my mother's every narcissistic whim, and when my father came out of the hospital, he wasn't anymore.

The trouble started with Tony. According to Betsy's version, when Tony was a toddler he wasn't the perfect child like Betsy. and my mother disciplined him. My father didn't like how she did it. That was the beginning of The War.

The end result of all this for me meant that every time my parents had an argument, my mother would come to me after and tell me it was because my father was crazy. It was not because he needed to defend us. She blamed it all on the psychiatrist, who 'gave him a lot of crazy ideas.' I heard this not one time, not a few times, but every single time they had a fight.

I never believed my mother about this but one cannot deny that it understandably created yet another internal conflict in me. My father was my protector. His energetic view infused my life, he was a towering figure of everything good in life to me.

What would it all mean if he were crazy? This was a frightening possibility to me. For me to even consider it felt like a betrayal.

When I was an adult, my mother told me another version, how when my father checked himself into the hospital, it was because he was afraid that he would hurt my mother. How she had a home and children to take care of, and she didn't have a car. The hospital wouldn't let her have it. After all, they said, my father wouldn't want her to have it if he felt like killing her. I have no reason to disbelieve her but knowing my mother, it could be an embellishment. In this case, I tend to think not. Either way, my grandfather - my mother's father - had to go to the hospital with my mother and make them give the car to her. And, of course, there was the shame of it. So later, I saw a different side of it. I saw how hard that must have been for her, and I came to feel some small pity and forgiveness.

Still, the idea of 'crazy Dad' became a fixture of my mother's truth in The War.

* * *

The War was about The Rules, surely starting when we kids had broken one of them, or my father had spent money, no matter how little. I guess by Sunday, when it was my father's second day home from work dealing with it, he would reach his limit. Thus began the ritual Sunday family fights.

The first fight I remember was when I was about three. Apparently, by then I knew that Mom could get in trouble if she was mean to the kids. She did something I didn't like, so when my father came home from work, I told him Mom was being a witch, and they had a fight. Afterwards, I felt guilty about it.

Most of the fights were about the kids except during the hard money years. My father would call my mother domineering, and say she was like her mother. I didn't know what that meant. I didn't know my grandmother well enough to determine if such a thing were true. She always seemed kindly to me. My father, on the other hand, was 'crazy,' although my mother usually waited until after the fight to say that. When they were fighting, she just wanted her way. There was something we were supposed to be doing, right? And she wanted that to be okay. So I guess my father was right. She was domineering.

Frequently during these fights, Tony, Chris and I would sit up on the stairs above my parents listening. They would be yelling so loudly that everyone was afraid the neighbors would hear them, my mother's shrill, high-pitched voice slicing through my father's bellowing. We would listen to my parents arguing about Mom being mean to us, with Dad jumping in to defend us. If Betsy were home, she wouldn't sit with us. She, after all, was always on my mother's side in family arguments. So Tony, Chris and I would sit there on those gold-carpeted stairs and listen for what seemed like hours. We didn't speak as we huddled there, frozen, mesmerized in a kind of confused, fascinated horror. Feeling righteousness for our cause but also feeling guilt over starting the fight, and feeling anxiety, especially if they were yelling about a getting a Divorce.

Eventually the fights would fizzle. and my mother would come looking for us to make Sunday dinner. Sunday dinner, when most of the time we would pretend nothing had happened, and my aunt would come over to eat with us and to give me my piano lesson, and life would go on.

* * *

My sister was spared most of this during her early formative years since The War didn't start until after my older brother was a toddler. By then, she was already ten. Mostly she was gone somewhere by then, if not to school, to relatives who were one place or another by the time the rest of us got a little older. This I know through oral history, mostly from Aunt Bobby, a more reliable source.

The War was mostly over when Chris was growing up. In a way, Chris was an afterthought. He was The Forgotten Child. I suppose many families have one, although in some ways, I think that was a good thing for him given my family. He wasn't under the same scrutiny as the rest of us.

So, Tony and I were the ones most caught up in the middle of The War: Tony, the Slightly-On-The-Outside child, and me, falling short of my sister's perfection. It was also because we were the rebellious ones, the ones causing all the trouble. I had the worst of that. Boys will be bad, they will sow their wild oats, and my brother was indeed a 'bad boy.' However, despite the challenges that bad boys present, bad boys are also dashing and daring and admirable in their own way. Bad girls, seemingly like me, are just bad.

* * *

And so, there were The Rules and The War and the burgeoning fault lines they birthed, and that was How It Began.

Mom and Dad, date unknown

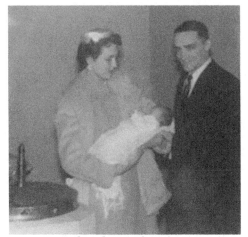

Mom and Dad at my baptism, 1959

Aunt Bobby, date unknown

*My mother and my brothers and I by the ubiquitous sewing machine, 1968.
Mom was clearly depressed.*

*My mother, Chris, Betsy and I, Christmas, 1967
Tony is absent, reason unknown.*

My mother and I on our way to a Mother-Daughter Breakfast at church, 1966
My sister was away at college.

CHAPTER 2

The World Outside

My family moved to the house I grew up in when I was a baby in 1960. The most important benefit of this house was that it was two blocks away from the Catholic Church, and with it, the Catholic school I would attend for eight years.

My sister never went to that Catholic school; she continued at the school she'd attended before we moved. I'm not sure why, as this seems odd; she was only eleven or twelve when we moved there. But my brother went to the school, Holy Family. I was three when he did. To say I was devastated when Tony went to school is an understatement.

During the week, Dad was away at work, and my mother was always busy. There was no time to play with children; there was always something that needed to be done. So it was that my brother was my company when I was very little. When my brother went to school, I remember sitting alone on the floor surrounded by toys. There was a feeling of wordless despair, and I was completely unable to play with them. This is the first feeling of depression I can remember.

I had another depression when I was young, or at least another mental health incident. That was when I was seven, when my mother's father died and my mother went to Florida to be with my grandmother. Despite the fact that I often resented my mother from a young age, I was also desperately attached to her. She would always say I was her clingiest child, and I don't doubt that is true. I'm not sure if I was born clingy, maybe I was, maybe I wasn't. And anyway, it doesn't matter if it was nature or nurture except that this statement from my mother was never a compliment. I guess 'clingy' is not one of those things you were supposed to be 'best' at.

I was in Second Grade when my mother went to Florida with my little brother for several months. She went to take care of my grandmother in April. The rest of that school year, I went to my Uncle Walter and Aunt Elsie's house and played with my cousins. Their house was a smaller house than ours, although there were ten of them. It had an odd, musty smell that I really couldn't place. I just knew it didn't smell like our house where the large open windows always swept the rooms with fresh air.

With my mother in Florida, my Aunt Elsie took care of me until my father came home. My sister was off doing Betsy things, I guess, and I don't remember if my older brother went with me. He would have been ten, so maybe he didn't need to.

My Uncle Walter, my mother's younger brother, was a solemn, silent presence, with a buzz haircut and large build. He was so unlike my father, and so unlike Aunt Bobby, for that matter. Aunt Elsie had straight hair that went white early. My mother could never understand why my aunt never chose to dye it, and thought this was rather scandalous. But Aunt Elsie wasn't vain like my mother, and always dressed in utilitarian clothes. She was kind to me while not physically affectionate. Years and years later, Aunt Elsie gave me a coloring she saved of Mickey Mouse that I had made exactly from that time, the time when my Granddaddy died.

Although I mostly enjoyed my time there, when I went home at night, I missed my mother. I remember she would call long distance on the telephone, which was a very big deal in those days, especially in my penny-pinching household. I remember my family being so excited when my mother called from Florida one day. They rushed to put me on the phone thinking how happy I'd be. But I felt an exquisite pain when I heard her voice, and I could say absolutely nothing. My father and sister were completely baffled because they thought I would be overjoyed. In adulthood, I came to call this place, this place of exquisite pain, "The Place with No Words".

Eventually the school year ended, and the situation must have seemed desperate, because one day my father and sister rushed to put me on a plane that I actually missed. I went on the plane the next day, and then everything was okay. Florida was my happy place, and I had my mother.

Later, someone in my family, maybe my sister, told me I had actually never let them turn the lights out at night while my mother was gone. I don't remember being scared at all, and I don't remember this occurrence, but in hindsight, I had obviously been in some kind of crisis. And that was because, despite my studied resistance against her from a young age, I desperately wanted my mother. That tug and pull, that resistance and want, became one of the deep and abiding paradoxes of my life.

* * *

When it was time for me to go to First Grade, Tony wouldn't take me, although he was going anyway because he was going there for his Fourth Grade. I remember Tony and my mother having a big fight about it. This was sad for me. The school was two blocks away and it was my first day of my first grade. Why wouldn't my mother be happy to take me? It never occurred to me then, but I remember feeling shattered that my brother could not bear to be with me.

It probably wouldn't have mattered so much if I had had a mother, but in her absence, my brother was my reality. So it mattered much more than it should have when I became his tag-along little sister. Because that is what I was by then. I was the annoyance and bother my brother did not want around.

I often wonder why Tony became like this, was it just the natural progression of kids growing older? Peer pressure? Maybe it was that. But one of the greatest fault lines in my family was beginning to show. After kindergarten, I was already ahead of Tony in school, although I have to say he wasn't dumb. He had an IQ well above average. It just wasn't enough to shine in my house. I think that's when he officially became the child who was 'Slightly On The Outside' in my family instead of holding his rightful place, his place as The Second Child. The fault line had emerged.

However it happened, I was definitely persona non grata to him for the next 15 years.

* * *

When I was forty-one, I went through a massive depression, the worst I ever had. Those were my Jungian therapy years, and I had a series of dreams. In many of them, I was a quadriplegic. Then I had hands that worked, but I was still in the wheelchair. In the dream, the doctor called me to come in in a rather urgent voice. He said I had had a terrible injury when I was young that had never healed that no one had ever even known about. When I went to the doctor's office, he told me I had broken my back when I was young, and no one had ever treated it. Then he took me in to see the x-rays. These turned out to be a series of pictures on the wall of my brother and I when we were little, one young age after another. In that series, you could see in each picture he was holding my hand. He was holding my hand in my baby picture, he was holding my hand in the next picture at age one and holding my hand in the next.

And then he wasn't.

So that's what had broken my back. Funny thing is, long after I had these dreams, I came across some old family photos taken before I had that memory, and that is exactly what I see.

That series of dreams was convoluted, as dreams often are, but it had a good ending. My father was alive, and I was a perfect little girl in a darling sky-blue jacket with a Peter Pan collar and big round buttons, and I was healthy. At least when my father was in the room. If I left that room where my father was, I was back in the wheelchair, but when I went back to my father, I wasn't.

So I needed my mother, and in our screwy little world, I needed my brother, too. But they didn't need me.

Thank God for Daddy.

* * *

At least by then, there was a world outside. As I said, I was a good student. We had nuns, and with a few exceptions, they were all very kindly. I liked all the other children at school, and I assumed they liked me. First Grade was sweet Sr. Rose Patricia. Second Grade was the holy terror Sr. St. Vincent. Third Grade was Mrs. Ferrin, who was very artistic, when to my chagrin, I found out I wasn't. Fourth grade was Mrs. Van Aken.

I was teacher's pet in Mrs. Van Aken's class. By this time, I also had glasses, cat glasses my mother picked out for me. I had told my mother for what seemed like a long while that I couldn't see, but she didn't believe me, not until I failed the eye exam at school. When she finally took me to the doctor, I couldn't even see the big E on the eye chart.

Mrs. Van Aken was very fond of me. I, in my little cat glasses in the hippie year of 1968, would stay after school and help her with her classroom, and with putting up decorations and things. She was always just a little amusingly befuddled, and it was fun to help her. Also, it helped that I didn't get in trouble for staying after school to help my teacher like I did when I went to my neighbors. I was 'doing something.'

All in all, school was a happy place for me.

* * *

I would be remiss if I overlooked the turmoil of our country during the 60s when I was growing up. What I remember most about the 60s is that they were loud. I heard loud music on my brother's radio, and loud people on TV when we watched the nightly news. Loud, loud, loud, everywhere and all the time.

Needless to say, the 60s were also violent and scary. One of my earliest memories is of the time when John F. Kennedy was shot. I was only four, and I don't remember John F. Kennedy, I only know what I've seen in videos later. However, I did know that the grown-ups were very upset, and so I was upset, too, and afraid. Afraid about people getting shot like that. If that could happen to the President, what would happen to the rest of us?

That was just the beginning. It seemed like there were always people getting shot. Bobby Kennedy. Martin Luther King. George Wallace. It seemed like a common occurrence, I almost expected it and was never surprised.

Then there were the Vietnam war protests. There was always some kind of protest going on when we watched the news at night, and college kids on campus were getting shot. People were screaming 'Pigs' at the cops. I just couldn't understand any of it. Weren't the cops the good guys?

I didn't understand the Vietnam War. I only knew that my father, the conservative who was perennially fighting the Cold War in his head, was in support of it. But it seemed like no one else was. People were burning American flags. That just didn't seem right to me, and in my own way, I felt hurt by it. This was my country after all, and even as a little girl, I loved it. Among other things, I was enormously proud that we'd landed men on the moon.

Of course, the mantra of the 60s anti-war movement became sex and drugs and rock and roll. This was also terribly confusing to me. I don't know that I ever really made sense of all of it. All I knew was that there were people acting in ways that to me seemed crazy, and I didn't like hard rock music. The Beatles were okay, I guess. I was also four when my sister excitedly gathered the whole family to watch The Beatles on the Ed Sullivan show. Personally, I didn't see what the big deal was.

People screaming about sex all the time was so much in conflict with what I heard in my own house. I just didn't know what to believe, but it did seem to me that maybe my parents were not entirely right about the pre-marital sex thing after all.

The drug use was particularly disturbing to me. Hearing stories about heroin was absolutely terrifying to me. I felt sorry for heroin addicts that died; Janis Joplin and a host of others. More death. Never even in my later years when I myself was using drugs myself did I ever consider using heroin. I was just too afraid of it.

There were other protests, women screaming about 'women's lib' and burning their bras. I couldn't understand this either. What was wrong with the way my mother lived? Now I look back and think that while it seemed extreme, this was absolutely necessary. I shudder to think about living my life constricted to being a housewife. Don't get me wrong, I loved the years when my children were little and I did this, but it was certainly never all I wanted to be. Sometimes extreme yelling is needed to be the catalyst for change, although that was not how I felt at the time. I wanted things to be the way it seemed to me they were meant to be, and that was the way things were.

Some of the biggest protests - riots even - were about race, and that came to roost even in my own back yard. I remember driving Downtown when I was little. My mother and I were going to see my Aunt Bobby in NW DC. We passed a place with many people that my mother referred to as Resurrection City. For history buffs, this was in 1968, and included a staged sit-in for protestors. It was more than that; people lived there. When we passed Resurrection City and my mother told me what it was, I was again confused. I asked my mother, "Is that like Resurrection Cemetery where my grandfather is buried?" My mother got a little disapproving frown on her face, and tersely said no. I don't know about my father, we never talked about it, but my mother, at least, was a racist.

Not that this was uncommon at all where I lived. We lived in a white neighborhood and avoided the ghettos of SW DC. The tides were turning though, and one day the neighbors behind us sold their house to a black family. 'They' had come to our neighborhood. The Italian lady who also lived behind us was furious. She was so angry that when she talked to the people who had sold their house, she spit on them. This became a big scandal in the neighborhood; it was all anyone talked about for days.

I had no real concept of the immensity of the racial problems in the US, but I do know the protests were very one-sided. Most of the protestors were black. I was enormously gratified that during the racial protests of 2020 after the horrendous murder of George Floyd, just as many white people joined the protests as black. Maybe things have not changed as much as they need to, but certainly they have changed some. It's a human problem now, not just a race one, and hopefully together, things will continue to change. We've at least come some ways from the day a little black girl just wanted to go to school but needed the National Guard to escort her. We still have a long way to go.

Of course, it's not the 60s anymore, and I'm not a child, but I'll always remember the 60s as an unhappy cocktail of violence, death, and unrest capped off with loud rock music that I never really liked.

* * *

Despite the turmoil of the larger world, my immediate little world didn't seem to change much in those days, so to whatever degree was possible, I was insulated. All the kids in my class had been together in the beginning of First Grade, and most were there at the end of the Eighth. I remember the first time a family moved off our street. I was totally shocked that could even happen because I didn't even know families could do that.

I had a crush on a boy in Fourth Grade, Danny. In my fairy tale eyes, he was a prince, the best boy in our class. Then there was Rosemary with her perfectly ironed uniform pleats and perfect ringlets of hair. And Christine, the class princess who sometimes walked to school with me. And, of course, there were other little Irish girls and other little Irish boys, and other little Italians. Sometimes the kids were mean, even me occasionally, but mostly I thought we were all happy. Still, I was competitive - I always had to be the best at everything. And win the prince. I was very vain, and anything less was an offense to my vanity. Not only was anything less an offense to my vanity, but it would also have broken The Rules. As for 'hanging out' with friends, mostly it wasn't my classmates I played with. I generally played with my neighbor, Karen A., who was four years younger than me. We became fast friends, at least until life changed.

***

And that was The World Outside.

"He was holding my hand, he was holding my hand, he was holding my hand... And then he wasn't."
The last picture is at my grandparent's house in FL. It's the last photo with Tony holding my hand, shortly before I became his pariah.

1969 - Silly me, the biggest nerd, although here I didn't know it yet I was still brilliantly sassy.

Happy girls in the schoolyard. I am second from left.

CHAPTER 3

The Extended Family

My father loved to sing. He would sing rousing songs at church, then at home he would sing and play rousing songs on his harmonica. He would play the Notre Dame fight song on his harmonica, and we, the youngest three of us anyway, would march around happily behind him. We'd have family parties, and my father would have a 'high ball' and bellow out German beer-drinking songs at the top of his lungs as everyone at the party sang along around my aunt playing the piano.

We had lots of parties. My grandparents, my mother's parents, were particularly fond of crab feasts. We would even have little parties when it was my grade's turn for the church bake sale. My mother would make her legendary coffee cake, which everyone in the neighborhood wanted, and then we would celebrate. Somewhere along the line, my grandparents had their golden wedding anniversary - that was the biggest party of all. For weeks we painted (cheap) little trinkets golden, and we invited all the cousins, and we had a big tent in the backyard. And there was lots of singing.

Even when I was very little, my father would sing to us. When we were tiny and Tony and I shared a room, at night, my father would come in and sing to us, but not usually lullabies.

He would sing *Camptown Ladies Sing that Song*, marching it all out, dancing around the room. Or songs that required us singing back, like *The Hole in the Bucket*, where we would start, "There's a hole in the bucket, dear Daddy, dear Daddy," and he would reply, "Well fix it, dear Regina, dear Regina, well fix it." That was followed by a series of interchanges about how to fix it until we ended up needing the bucket to fix it. Or *The Hole in the Bottom of the Sea*, with the hole in the bottom of the sea, with a log in the hole in the bottom of the sea, then the bump on the log, then the frog on the bump on the log and on and on. Not sure how that frog was breathing at the bottom of the sea. A particular favorite was *The Old Lady Who Swallowed a Fly*. She has a series of misadventures where she swallows larger and larger animals to catch the little ones, until she swallows a horse. Too bad for the old lady, it didn't end well for her.

But there were sad songs, too, like *Ol' Man River*. Dad would be singing, and all the while acting it out for us, pulling the log, toting the bale, and waving his hands to the rolling waves of the river.

The saddest nightly song was *The Whiffenpoof Song*. It was an old Bing Crosby wartime song that I can only describe as a poignant seeking. My father would stare out the window sadly and sing, this time with no acting:

> *"Gentleman songsters off on a spree*
> *Doomed from here to eternity*
> *Lord have mercy on such as we*
> *Baa, baa, baa..."*

When I was little, I never knew what made my father so sad when he sang that song. Now I think that, in later life, it was my father's only reference to his own father. To his alcoholic father, who committed suicide and became doomed to hell by the Catholics, and who beat his mother. The father he never talked about.

* * *

There was one place in my childhood where I was always happy, and that was Florida. My grandparents, my mother's parents, moved from DC near where I grew up to Lake Worth, FL. Later in life, I heard a fabulous story about it. Apparently, when my grandparents first got married, long before this, before their children were born, before there was even electricity, my grandparents lived in Lake Worth. They didn't have a house; they lived in a tent on the beach and would collect oysters to eat, marvelously in love with each other. How very unconventional of them, how deliciously bohemian! Heaven knows how my mother turned out the way she did. My grandparents moved from Florida when my aunt was born to be with my grandfather's family in Wisconsin - a terrible trade, in my opinion. In any event, when I was very young, they went back to Lake Worth.

Every year, we would travel to Lake Worth and spend two weeks there with many adventures, and some misadventures. Often, Aunt Bobby would fly down to meet us. These trips were wonderful. Not just because of the beautiful, sunny palm trees and searing heat, although I loved both. It was because in that house, in that place, in that time, there were no Rules, and there was no War, and there were no chores, and there were no fights, and we were free.

***

I don't remember much about my grandparents, I was only seven when my grandfather died and eight when my grandmother died. My grandfather was an affable old soul: tall, sturdily built with thick, wavy white hair, with whom my father got along well. My grandmother was Irish, slightly heavy and quite gray as she was almost eighty by the time I remember her. She was actually eight years older than my grandfather. My grandfather wasn't Irish; he was a mix of German Swiss and who knows what else, a Catholic by conversion.

From what I do know of my mother's family, it seemed the world centered around my grandfather. My grandmother's world did, my mother's world did, my aunt's world did. I dare say my aunt never got over when my grandfather suddenly died of colon cancer. He was seventy-four. My grandmother passed shortly after, she died of a broken heart. They were buried up here with us in Maryland, and every Sunday when the weather was nice, Aunt Bobby would take me to the cemetery. We would pack up homegrown daffodils and irises, and go to a field of rolling graves with inset headstones. The cemetery was built on the beautiful grounds of what used to be Lord Baltimore's mansion. My aunt and I would feed the ducks, I always liked that. My mother never came. I think she couldn't take it, couldn't take the reminder, couldn't manage the grief. When my grandfather got sick, I remember my mother on the telephone, and then I remember her crying afterward. It was the only time in my life I saw my mother cry. I was alone with her, and I was seven, and I was helpless. There was that exquisite pain.

* * *

In all, there were four siblings in my mother's family, two boys and two girls. Aunt Bobby was the eldest and never married. Since not getting married was literally the worst thing that could happen to you, in my mother's eyes, my aunt was a failure. My aunt never realized what a scapegoat she was, or if she did, maybe she thought she deserved it. Aunt Bobby was like that in ways. She took a lot of abuse from my mother, mostly because of her weight. It was part of the Sunday ritual. My aunt would come for dinner, and for my piano lesson, and to sometimes participate in the ritual Sunday family fight, and to listen to my mother berate her for whatever she was eating. What did it matter? Except obviously, that's what led my aunt to her cardinal sin: being unmarried.

My mother's brother, Uncle Walter, had married and had eight children. Aunt Bobby always hated my Uncle Walter's wife, Elsie. During the ritual Sunday visits, we would hear about Aunt Bobby's latest foray to my Uncle Walter's house on her way to ours. I guess hate is a strong word. Aunt Bobby was deeply hurt because she felt Aunt Elsie had taken my uncle away from them, from that idyllic sibling family. I dare say Aunt Bobby never got over that, at least not until they were old, when all the men were dead and gone anyway.

My other uncle, Uncle Erv, was tall, taller than my father and Uncle Walter, and slim. Even when I was grown, he could wrap me up in a big hug as if he were an envelope, and I would feel safe and warm and protected.

Uncle Erv didn't get married until late in life. Not sure why, but my mother forgave him for this. She idolized him. He was brilliant, like my father, and had a presence. You knew you were in a presence when you were with him, and most importantly, he knew you were there with him. He was an architect and a science fiction writer. One of his short stories ended up being published in a short story anthology *The World's Best Science Fiction, 1969*, right there next to Isaac Asimov and Ray Bradbury. This was a point of particular pride for my mother, who needed everyone to be the best at everything. Maybe that's the reason my mother forgave my uncle for being unmarried, although she also had different standards for boys because they did not so closely reflect on her, so maybe he didn't so badly need to be married.

The story Uncle Erv wrote is of note, called *HEMEAC*. It's about a person needing to belong, a person with ancient fears, a person struggling in an aging, decrepit system built on a twisted sense of perfection; a person hoping not to be thrown to the savages for some small, mysterious infraction. A person judging those outside the system as terrifying, because that's what he was taught. The ending of the story is tragic and poignant, and entirely unexpected. I won't spoil it. You can still find it on Goodreads fifty years later. Good stories never die.

Was it a metaphor for the Catholic Church? When I got older, I thought so, but by then my uncle was dead and I couldn't ask him.

When my grandparents died, my Uncle Erv moved into their Florida house. He was in his forties and still single. My family and I still went to Florida every year, now to see him, until I was fifteen. When Uncle Erv eventually did get married - to an ex-nun no less - my new aunt had had enough of us staying with them. So on the very last visit, we stayed at a motel and then we never went back there again. But to this day, in my secret mind's eye, I can still smell the sweet, musty smell of that beautiful little house, with its grapefruit tree in the yard, and its orange tree, and the gardenias. Citrus and sweet gardenias. I once wrote a poem about that.

* * *

My closest cousins were the ones who lived in my neighborhood, Uncle Walter's children, who went to the same school. There were six boys and two girls in that family. Most were older than me, like my sister. There was one girl my sister's age, and one girl my age; I guess a happy coincidence.

There was Walter John, whom I hardly knew, and Anton, whom my aunt would take me to see when he got married. Then there was Mark. I was in madly love with my older cousin Mark. Mark was alive. He was joyous. I would watch with glee as he would dance Russian leg dances down the street, and he would sing and sing and sing.

Then came Danny, or DJ as he came to be called, who smoked marijuana with us at my sister's wedding. There was Christine, my sister's age, my slightly-older cousin Eric, my closest cousin Katherine, and their youngest brother, Steven.

I don't know when half of those children realized they were gay, the great crime of the age. Four of them died of AIDS, although Walter John said he got it from IV drug use as he was an addict. I knew that at young age, Eric was different. The neighborhood children would make fun of him and call him a fag. It was a heartbreak to the family due to the times we were in when they lived. The scandals, and the shunning, and the deaths.

Mark was the first to go, and his funeral was very hush-hush. We hadn't seen him in years, although I think he had made peace with his parents by then. When Danny died after caring for Mark, and after I was already sober, I cried and played piano and sang *Danny Boy* over and over at the top of my lungs until eventually I was tired, and blessed sleep came. Eric just disappeared, as did Walter John and Anton, who may have died from complications of alcoholism.

I was so in awe of Mark that I don't remember registering my cousin Kathy until I was in Eighth Grade. Well, we always called her Kathy when we were growing up;, my children call her 'Laffy Kathy' to this day. But for whatever reason, she's Katherine now, and I respect her wishes. She was a year behind me in school. Katherine grew tall and has the German Swiss build of her father, her hair going white young like her mother's did. I mostly love her dimples, and her expansive, infectious laugh. Katherine was in awe of Mark, too.

By the time I got to my better years in late high school, we became fast friends, and still are today.

* * *

Of course, there was another side of the family, my father's side. My father's family lived in Detroit, MI, in the heyday of that town. My grandmother - my father's mother - was there, and my father's brother-in-law and his sister, Uncle Louie and Aunt Irene, and their four children. My cousins were all much older than me, several even older than my sister. The girls had that glamorous, exotic Italian beauty that my sister had. The oldest one had a daughter my age, Lisa, and she was my Detroit companion.

One of the most important things about my aunt and uncle and their family, at least according to my mother, was that they were rich. It was a bonus 'best' if you will. They lived in a glamorous house in Grosse Point, with a grand, spiraling staircase and perfectly decorated children's bedrooms with every single Nancy Drew book. Although everyone in my grandfather's family had started in tile and terrazzo, my uncle invested his money in his own company that made car parts when cars were made in Detroit, and he made a fortune.

Despite that, my grandmother lived quite modestly and I'm sure she wanted it that way. Grandma Nona, as she was called, was a forbidding soul who spoke Italian and only broken English. I didn't understand most of what she said because we didn't speak Italian at my house, my mother being Irish-German-Swiss. I only have a few memories of my Grandma Nona.

Once was when I was playing in her garden, she got angry because I wandered off the stepping bricks. Once I wanted to play after I ate, and evidently it was very important that you wait a half hour for your food to digest before you could ever do something like that. But I rarely stayed with Grandma Nona or with my aunt and uncle. I stayed with my Detroit companion, Lisa. Lisa was the daughter of my oldest cousin, Angie, and was only a year younger than me.

As on my mother's side, in Michigan, I had a cousin I adored - Cousin Louie (to differentiate from my Uncle Louie). He was the youngest, and closest to my age. He would teasingly sing, "Little Regina, don't be meana," and "Tony Baloney, don't be phony," and we would all laugh hysterically.

But Lisa was my closest cousin, being my age, though first cousin once removed, and I would stay at her house with her parents and their other two daughters. It's hard to describe Lisa. Lisa was a crazy spark, with blonde hair and a mischievous smile, and she was always coming up with wild ideas for adventures. It was unfortunate the time I went there when her family went to the Bahamas for Christmas. I took it very personally, but my aunt bought me a spirograph, an inexplicable luxury, and so I managed.

But we were indeed the poor ones, though we weren't poor, only in comparison. Another Christmas when we went to celebrate at their house, my mother carted all our Christmas presents up to Michigan to give to us. My cousin Lisa got what I can only call dazzling presents. My uncle, her grandfather, had bought her a whole toy mini-kitchen, and who knows what else. As I sat there amazed at this bounty, I started to open my presents where I discovered that I, my mother being my mother, had gotten me socks. There again in my life was The Place With No Words.

When we were teenagers, Lisa would abscond with my uncle's fancy car without permission, and we'd drive around wildly and drink a few beers. There were always adventures like this. At my Cousin Louie's wedding, which was a lavish affair at a country club where we all stayed together for three days, we were sneaking cigarettes that I hid in my puffy sleeves. This worked well until my cousin Louise tapped me on the shoulder and caught us.

Louie and Louise. Yes, my uncle who was Louis had a son named Louis and also a daughter named Louise. I guess one namesake wasn't enough, or when they had Louise, maybe they thought they would never have a boy. They were on their third girl when Louise was born. My uncle quite obviously had a big ego. Later my cousin Louise said she thought my uncle had bipolar disorder, but I was never close enough to see it.

Though she was a little untamed, Lisa always had a good heart. Then, to her great surprise, she got pregnant in college. Lisa married the father and made a family with three children. I heard she became a social worker, though we lost touch after my father died. But she was rich, and went to fancy country clubs, and rode in fast cars. Lisa had a lucky bonus; she had dear Cousin Louie all of the time.

Many years later, my cousin Louise, the Italian family story-keeper, relayed that Lisa couldn't stop drinking, which was saying a lot because drinking was rampant in that family. Eventually, Lisa died. Lisa-of-the-dazzling-toys was dead at the age of fifty-one from complications of alcoholism.

My Cousin Louie, per cousin Louise, was also bipolar and at some point, he took over the family business from my uncle. Apparently, in a manic moment, Cousin Louie put all of the family fortune into an investment recommended by his brother-in-law. That investment cost the family everything. They lost every single stinking penny. Fortunately, most of the others had their own sources of income by then.

Cousin Louie's wife, a nice lady, sipped sherry all day instead of eating (you absolutely had to be thin as well as rich) until her stomach digested itself. She died at forty-four. They had eight children.

My Uncle Louie and my Aunt Irene both committed suicide later in life. My uncle became mortally ill. He was in a lot of pain and couldn't take it anymore. My aunt, my father's sister who was not herself ill, joined my uncle in this suicide pact as she didn't want to live without him.

For all their glamorous lives, in the end, even the rich ones were not exempt from the family mental illness or addictions.

* * *

The mental illness and addiction did not stop with my generation. Although my sister's children haven't had an issues, two of mine have. My youngest, Patrick, suffers from anxiety and depression. In one two year period, he was hospitalized for mental health issues six times. He is better now, thankfully. He is on disability but he is well self-educated and a good person.

My middle son, David, another Second Child, suffers from Bipolar I disorder and addiction both. As sweet as he is, we have been through hell and back again together. Hospital after hospital, jail after jail. Methamphetamines, opioids, alcohol, spice, marijuana. Many times I thought he would die, but that's a story for another book. Right now, but for who knows how long, he is clean and mentally stable. He lives in a group home for people with mental health issues.

With my children, I take the good days as they come, and gird myself for the future.

* * *

Thus was the world of The Extended Family, a world where the family curse was always lurking in the shadows, no one ever knowing when it would strike.

My paternal grandparents and my father and my aunt in the early 1920s
My paternal grandfather was and always will be a myth to me.

My forbidding paternal grandmother with Mom, Dad, and me

*My maternal grandmother and me in Florida.
I have no pictures of my maternal grandfather.*

*Tony and me with our cousins closest in age, Eric and Katherine in their backyard.
From left to right, Tony, myself, Eric and Katherine*

Katherine and I grown

Glamorous Cousin Louie and me

Lisa-of-the-dazzling-toys, dead at fifty-one
I always thought Lisa had it better than me, but even so, I always loved her,
Wild-child that she was.

Cousin Danny, victim of AIDS
"Oh Danny boy, the pipes, the pipes are calling…"

CHAPTER 4

The Beginning of The End of Believing in Fairytales

One sunny autumn day when I was in Sixth Grade, I put on my little Catholic school uniform and walked the two short blocks to my school into the school yard where we assembled until the nuns rang the bell. The school yard where we had already gathered for nigh on six years, where we played hopscotch, and jumped rope, and swung on a tire swing. Where we teased David Showers (it was a curse if you got 'Shower's Cooties' in Second Grade), and where I nurtured my abiding love for the class prince, Danny, at least from the Fourth Grade.

When I got to school, there was a ruckus in the yard. One of the girls was crying. As I was generally a kind person, I went over to see if I could help. There I got the first shock of my adolescence. Cindy was crying. She was sobbing. It was heartbreaking. Unbeknownst to me, the reason she was crying was me.

Cindy was crying because she was going to have a slumber party, and because our mothers were friends, her mother was making her invite me. That was when I found out I was a nerd - beyond that, a pariah. This was an earthquake for me. The world was changing. It was 1969, and it was the year of hippies. Certainly, my cat glasses, my status as teacher's pet, my school excellence, and probably my condescending vanity about it was disqualifying for me, although I hadn't known it.

For whatever reason, even to this day I do not understand why, I went to that party though all the kids teased me about it. Maybe I just couldn't believe that these friends of mine, these people I had known all through school, would actually be mean to me. Maybe this was all some sort of mistake, an imaginary twisting of reality like some sort of mirror at the carnival funhouse.

So I dressed up. I had new one-inch high heels, and I went. Again at the party, Cindy was crying. There was one girl there I had been friends with to some degree for a long time, Christine. I walked to school with her sometimes. I was vaguely aware that she might have had some kind of relationship with my prince, but that didn't really register with me. At the party, Christine gave me a note, and as if it were my fairytale, it was from my hero, Danny. He wanted to be with me. I was in heaven for the rest of the night, it was so wonderfully amazing to me! I was walking on air.

The next day, after the slumber part of the party, we all went to church, and that's when I found out. I found out, after all, the note from Danny was all a joke, and the joke was on me.

Afterwards, we went back to Cindy's house and some of the boys came over, and that's when I heard one of them on the telephone laughing hysterically about it. My humiliation was complete.

* * *

Subsequent to this event, I found out that there were three tiers of people in my class, the king and queenly tier of Christine and Danny, the middle tier of those who were not quite good enough to be in the first tier but were still quite respectable, and the bottom tier, the losers like me.

But still I was optimistic. I decided to have my own party, and I invited all the first-tier kids. Surprisingly, my mother let me. We got off-brand snacks, and off-brand Coke; that was the way of it in my house. We couldn't spend much money on something that wasn't considered a real necessity. And then we waited. And waited. And waited …

And nobody came.

Afterwards, when my mother and I talked about it, there was no sympathy. A sub-rule of being pretty, I guess, meant you were also supposed to be popular. What I heard was my mother telling me, "No one would have ever done that to Betsy. Everyone always liked Betsy." And on and on about Betsy she went. So I had broken another of The Rules, and I hadn't lived up to Betsy, and I was alone.

For whatever reason, I didn't expect my father to solve that for me. I don't think he ever knew.

Much of what happens next is very jumbled. I started smoking because it was cool and Tony did it. I went to parties with the losers. One was wild Veronica, the oldest child in what I now know was an extremely dysfunctional family. She later went on to have big boobs, and then it stopped mattering to those outside our little Catholic school world that she was in the third tier. There was Margaret who would come to those third-tier parties, whose uncle I much later dated, and she was really weird. But looking back, she was very creative, and maybe creative was just weird.

But I was actually friends with a girl from the second and respectable tier, Eileen. She lived in a tiny duplex on the other side of the school, the other side of the tracks, and was one of six kids. When we were in Ninth Grade, her father died of alcoholism. It turns out he had beaten his sons for years. I don't know if Eileen was sad about it then or not, although we were still friends.

In the meantime, I tried and tried to figure out why Eileen was respectable while I was such a pariah, and decided it was the glasses, so I stopped wearing them outside of school even though I could not see. Remember? Not even the big E on the eye chart. I couldn't even recognize kids I knew when we hung out at the mall, but that didn't stop me. No more glasses for me.

**

One thing you needed to have to be cool in Sixth Grade was a bra. The kids would come up behind me and run their fingers down the back of my shirt, heaven forbid I didn't have one. I still hadn't bloomed in that regard, and really never did, as I was flat-chested like my mother. So when I asked my mother for a bra, she said no. Again, my mother would never buy something we didn't really need.

So I started on the adventure of stealing my mother's bras to prepare for that dreaded moment when the kids would be onto me. A little later, I began my extensive shoplifting career paired with my buddy Veronica who was already good at it. The first thing we stole for me was a bra. Veronica-with-the-big-boobs laughed at the double-A cups, and even those were too big for me. Shortly after that, when I started my period, I didn't tell my mother. I guess I was afraid, but she couldn't tell me I didn't need something for it, could she? Still, stealing seemed like the best option for me. I became so self-conscious that when, for whatever reason, we went to a public restroom with friends, I couldn't pee. Funny, it took my oldest son to tell me later that this is called 'shy bladder,' and he had it, too, so it's really a thing.

* * *

Eventually, by Seventh Grade, I made another second-tier friend, Tina. Her other friend, Karen W., took dancing, and was in a drum and baton corps that I joined until I was fifteen. I was quite clumsy, so I wasn't a respectable baton twirler. I was only a flag bearer, but it was good enough for me. Tina's parents were divorced because of her father's alcoholism. This was scandalous back then, however my mother somehow managed to overlook it.

But even that friendship was fraught with a tug-and-pull, the tug-and-pull for Tina. Karen W. wanted Tina for herself. She certainly didn't want to share Tina with me, nor even really be friends with me. She would always walk by Tina with me always on the other side. Never did I ever get to be the middle child in that threesome, and this again was my failure. Then when Tina and I had a big end-of-the-world fight, in despair I went and hid in the formal, gold-laden church sanctuary. That is, until the nuns and my father came to find me. I lay on the floor in the sanctuary for several hours in dramatic despair.

Maybe God would save me.

Later, Tina and Karen W. both wanted to be friends with me on Facebook. I friended Tina, but when she got sober, she got wildly religious and it was too much for me. I unfollowed her, but stayed friends. Karen W. can go fuck herself.

***

Even before I hit adolescence, there was always the sense that I was different. I'm not sure when it started, but once I was in school, I felt that way.

First off, I had a name teachers could never pronounce. Every school year when I went to the first day of a new class, my new teacher would take roll. There was always that moment of embarrassment when I would sit with my cheeks blushing as the teacher would try and try to say my name right. It was bad enough that I couldn't be a 'normal' Karen or Sue, but saying my last name was for some reason always a challenge. These embarrassing moments stretched interminably for me.

I also lived in a house that was different than everyone else's. I loved the house we lived in, and I appreciate it now all the more, but my uncle had designed it and it was different from everyone else's. I always found it awkward when kids would go by and make fun of it.

Even in little things, we were different. We didn't eat normal food. I would go to my neighbors where everyone else would drink whole milk and eat lunchmeat sandwiches. I wondered why at my house, we drank skim milk from a powder, and at our house, we had to eat liverwurst and Velveeta cheese. Liverwurst and Velveeta cheese was disgusting, I considered it the worst of the worst.

Of course, I always had the nagging sense that my mother was different, even though I couldn't necessarily articulate it or understand it's impact. My life was just different.

Feeling different, even under the best of circumstances

(which mine obviously weren't), has an impact on you. It forever marks you as an outsider. I was always on the outside looking in, and this feeling persisted well into adulthood. This made my adolescent challenges all the more difficult.

* * *

Tony was the hippiest, coolest hippie you've ever seen. He was the highly advanced age of fourteen. His hair was long, and he had a girlfriend, and lots and lots of friends. Of course, Tony continued to ridicule me as he had always done since First Grade. He would hang with his girlfriend and their Camelot court. They would go and sit on his girlfriend's porch where I would hear them laughing at me as I went by, riding my bike to the store to get candy.

* * *

In those days, and in many times since, I kept a diary. I never knew what happened to any of them. I guess I didn't care, because one day my sister and mother found one of them when they were moving. They said, "We never knew you were so depressed." I was good at hiding it in defiant rebelliousness. My sister told me she thought the diary was so depressing that I wouldn't want to see it, so she threw it away. I was offended by that; how did they know that there weren't things in there that I would have wanted to see? Although there probably weren't, but it wasn't their decision to make.

    The people who really didn't want to see it were my sister and mother. They would never want anyone to be reminded of any depression or failure or bad times in my family, even though it was twenty years gone behind.

* * *

So there I was in the third tier, sometimes managing to fool at least some people enough to sneak into the second.

    It was The Beginning of The End of Believing in Fairytales, although it wasn't the end. My world, The World Outside, had changed, and it would never again be the same.

Class Photo circa 1971.
By this time, I was no longer sassy, and wore no glasses even though I couldn't see.

CHAPTER 5

The End of Believing in Fairytales

When I was eleven, and that's how I remember it, although it was also Sixth Grade, my exalted brother took an interest in me again. He was fourteen. Little did I know what disaster lay ahead for me. I was happy.

It started with some compliments, I guess. You might even call it flirting. 'Grooming' they would call it these days. Then it progressed to some fondling of my breasts. This didn't seem all that strange to me, there had been other 'playing doctor' incidents in my childhood. Still, it was confusing. There was a natural curiosity and there was my deep need for Tony, my first love, to love me. At the same time, there was an inherent sense of wrongness because Tony was my brother, and because of my mother's obsession about no pre-marital sex. I felt hesitant, emotionally scratchy, but in the end, the curiosity and my need for Tony's love far outweighed any other considerations.

Tony's grooming went on for a period of weeks. Then one day, Tony made a suggestion. He suggested that we do what grown-ups do and have sex. I personally didn't know what that meant, but it didn't sound too bad to me. He explained what would happen, and when he did, I pictured my little brother's tiny floppy penis, how bad could that be? So we made arrangements to meet in his room at a specific time. It must have been when the rest of the family was going to be out of the house, we couldn't risk anyone walking in on us.

So at the appointed time, I dutifully showed up. Nothing could have prepared me. There he was sitting naked in all his glory, his excitement already showing. "Wait! This isn't what I signed up for! It was supposed to be little like Chris!" I didn't say that, but that's what I was thinking. Or rather, it became a yelling in my head, an internal scream. I went into what I can only call shock, moving in a world of the surreal, movements appearing in slow motion, walls bending in the reflected light, voices, both mine and Tony's, echoing tinnily from a distance.

Tony must have sensed my discomfort because he went on to reassure me. There was more petting and flirting, and a trip to my most private spots. This unleashed powerful erotic feelings in me that were overwhelming and utterly hypnotic. I was transfixed. So I stayed.

Things went on for a bit, and then it was time to do The Thing. We stood then with me facing the wall, a sickly pale green as I remember it. My brother tried to penetrate me as I faced the wall. Something must have gone horribly wrong because we didn't fit. He kept trying. Eventually, his parts went into my parts in the wrong way, and there was anal penetration. I immediately stiffened sharply, a jagged rigor overcoming my body. It didn't really hurt physically, at least that's not what I remember most about it. It just felt grossly overpoweringly wrong in some deeply primal way. That's when I snapped out of it. That's when I left, fumbling with my clothes and running away.

I don't really remember what I did after that. I do remember thinking that we had not been successful because there was something wrong with me, and that I was deformed in some terrible way. This meant I would never have babies. Like my dear friend, Diane, always says to me, "It's not about what happens to you. It's about how you feel about it." And not having babies was a death sentence. I wanted a baby. A baby would love me, like my kitten did.

I coupled that thinking with remembering how much

trouble my mother had had getting pregnant with me, and how she and I didn't have any breasts, which I must have known about from my other adventures in Sixth Grade by then, and that further confirmed the conclusion. No babies.

The other feeling I had was guilt that I had been a willing participant. That was breaking one of the biggest Rules, the one about being virginal. I was a bad girl, and given the unsuccessful nature of what had happened with Tony, I was not even good at being bad. Yet somewhere in my heart, there had been an innocent.

Not in all ways because of my mother, but in some ways, up to this moment, my spirit had been pure and clear just like the ripples of a freshwater brook running through the woods, gurgling cheerfully in the sun peeking through the trees. After, it felt like I had been forever sucked into a horrifying void of ink-black darkness, a world where I forever felt shadowy, a world where I felt lost and ashamed and afraid and alone.

* * *

I never told anyone about what happened with Tony. It just became another secret, a hidden mountainous boulder always causing me to look away. Certainly, I couldn't tell my mother, and you didn't talk to Dad about stuff like that. There was no one else to tell. I just went my merry way, drawing my own conclusions. My brother went back to being mean to me. In fact, the worst of it was yet ahead. What had happened to me was terrible. What would happen later would be a tragedy.

There was one other incident I remember, and that was my first kiss. I don't remember when it was in relation to this, but I do know it was my brother. Do you know that one of those dumb questions they ask you to use when you verify your accounts online is to put in, "Who was your first kiss?" My first kiss was my brother. We were at a family friend's one day, and Tony decided he was going to teach me to kiss. It was a French kiss, and I remember I wasn't very good at it when he was instructing me. But I knew this just wasn't the way it was supposed to be. It was certainly not the way I had imagined my first kiss would be.

* * *

The worst thing in this period of my life was yet to happen, and it wasn't physical. Remember that this was all going on around the same time that my peers were soundly rejecting me. One day, I was getting ready to go out to see some friends, probably the second-tier ones. We had a full-length mirror hanging on the coat closet door. I used to get ready to go out and then stand in the mirror and make an assessment. Was I pretty enough to do it? So one particular day, I was standing in the mirror, and in spite of everything, in spite of Cindy's party, and in spite of me being deformed and never having any babies, I thought I looked pretty good. I was standing there for a while. It takes time to make such an assessment, right? Then Tony walked by. As he walked by, he said, "No one will ever love you; you have skinny ankles."

The fracture this statement created in me is indescribable. It was as if a flash-bang grenade had been casually tossed into my psyche. The explosion left an irreparable blankness in my spirit, a blankness stunned beyond emotion, a blankness that became an unshakable belief.

No one would ever love me.

Why did Tony say that? I do not know, although I have heard other incidents where after the sexual abuse, the emotional abuse follows. Maybe from subconscious guilt? I think it must be so.

* * *

In my mind, until right now this minute, this wasn't incest. Such an ugly word. It wasn't, was it? I've always called it sexual abuse, at least after I got sober and acknowledged it. After all, he wasn't really my brother, at least not a biological one. But now I see he was indeed my brother, and due to the lack of motherly love when I was a baby, even more. Although that burden, compensating for a missing parent, should not have been his burden to bear.

To this day, even the two times I have ever broached the topic with my brother since we were adults, he has never apologized although I've forgiven him. Children always forgive their abusers, right? They just want to get the love they didn't get but still need. I've made excuses again and again due to the hard life he had. He never had to apologize because he couldn't. He couldn't help it. He wasn't dealt a fair hand. He was jealous of me because of The Rule he was always failing at, the one about school, and I wasn't. He needed the second place, to be The Second Child, and I had taken it.

He himself was a victim of other things, I much later found out from my mother when I finally went to therapy. But he could have said he was sorry, couldn't he? He could have grown up and been a man and taken responsibility for it. His life might have worked out much better for him that way.

Or better yet, maybe I could have just had a nice brother, and maybe I could have just had nice people at school.

* * *

After all these events in Sixth Grade, including both my peer interactions and my brother, I knew what my life would be like. For me, there would never be some awkward, fumbling-but-romantic first kiss with a handsome prince. No lifelong friends from First Grade. No babies to love. These things were out of reach for me.

Even more importantly, I was breaking the all The Rules, all The Rules that applied outside the house. Breaking the virginal rule. Breaking the pretty rule. Breaking the popular rule. Knowing deep in my heart of hearts that no one would ever love me. Knowing that not only was I alone, but I would always, always be alone, and so I was breaking the final, final, most important rule of all, because no one would ever marry me.

* * *

And that was The End of Believing in Fairytales.

Would that I could have zoomed over it.

But I didn't. Instead, I started drinking and using drugs. By then, I was turning twelve.

Tony at his wedding when he was eighteen
At the time, I thought Tony was so handsome, but as I look at it today, I rather find it quite disturbing.

Tony later in life.
Tony and I have been on good terms since I was in my 20s

CHAPTER 6

Drugs and the End of Drugs

I preface this chapter, and the following chapters, with the following disclaimer:

For a long time after I got sober, I said, and truthfully thought, that my drinking was because of my mother. My close friends knew a bit more about the things in addition to my mother. Certainly, there was good enough reason to justify drinking. I really was a broken child, a broken pre-person shall we say, by the time I was twelve.

Then, at an AA meeting once, a man rudely stated that this opinion was bullshit. "We drink because we are alcoholics." I took some time to process that and saw his point. One time after I got sober, I was having an allergy attack and I took some of my kids' liquid Benadryl with a nice dose of alcohol in it. That was a wild experience. I remember driving, and every cell in my body was tingling, right to the tips of my fingers and toes, all the while my body screaming, "Give me more, give me more, give me more!" (Fortunately for me, this incident didn't lead to anything worse!)

That feeling of 'give me more' is called 'the phenomenon of craving.' It doesn't happen to non-alcoholics, but it does happen to any alcoholic who puts alcohol in their body. That's the difference between normal people and me, though I know it is hard for some people to understand it. So then I decided the rude man was right, and I started to say, "I drank because I am an alcoholic," instead.

Some people who might become alcoholics have the sense to recognize that feeling of craving, and since they aren't self-destructive, know enough to stay away from it. But for self-destructive people like me, it was the ticket to something, at least it was the ticket to somewhere to be, and that was oblivion.

I don't remember the first time I got drunk. I do remember stealing beers from my father's supply and drinking Rolling Rock beer and Boone's Farm wine very early on in my drinking career. That was partly to be cool. Tony was drinking and using drugs, and I wanted to be cool like him. But I'm sure at some point I drank enough to get 'that feeling,' and I loved it. I can't say alcohol made me happy, per se, but it certainly was the perfect escape from, as one of my friends used to wryly say, "The tragedy that is my life."

Now I think both opinions are true. I did drink because I was broken, and I drank because I hated myself. But I also drank alcoholically because I was experiencing the phenomenon of craving and I am an alcoholic. Either way, there is no doubt I became a hopeless drunk.

There was a man in AA, actually a man who was the father of one of my high school classmates. He used to say there were three stages of alcoholism: 'dizzy and delightful,' 'drunk and disorderly,' and 'dead drunk.' I used to add in my head ' then dead,' because I am sure I was trying to drink myself to death like the guy in the movie *Leaving Las Vegas*. Certainly, my drinking career included a lot of 'dead drunks,' especially in the final six years of it.

* * *

The first sign of trouble for me was Karen A., the Karen who lived across the street, the daughter at my neighbor's house. I liked their family. When they eventually moved, I was very stricken by it, and I would have dreams of being at their house. Mrs. A. tells a story to this day about one time when they had gone out.

When they came home, they found me there. I had let myself in their unlocked door, unlocked doors being the way of it then. I asked them why they had gone out without me. I was probably pretty young then, maybe eight years old. I don't remember this, but I'm sure it is true. I must sheepishly admit, I'm a little demanding that way to this very day.

I spent many hours at my neighbors' house playing with Karen. Life was different at her house. There were none of the tensions at her house that I experienced in mine, and none of the demands. The neighbors' basement wasn't like our basement. It was still sectioned like ours, but half of it was set up just for playing. Imagine that! It was there that we played with Karen's Ken and Barbie's. We twirled our batons to the music of the Associations and we danced our little hearts out, and life was carefree.

I was happy over at my neighbor's house until the dreaded phone would ring and it would be my mother looking for me. I think my neighbors would dread it, too. At a minimum, I'm sure they felt sorry for me.

Karen and I had played together since she was three perhaps, and I was seven. So by the time I was 12, we had been best friends for five years. Then I abandoned her. After all, she wasn't in the first tier of popularity at my school, or in the second tier; she wasn't even in my grade. Playing with Karen was totally uncool.

Today I know that my refusal to play with Karen anymore was hard for her to understand and it hurt her, though I don't know how badly. But I desperately needed to survive, and that survival didn't include her. Although I had enjoyed our time together and would miss Karen, my need for survival overshadowed everything I felt for her.

In hindsight, I see that my break with Karen was the first step on the long road ahead for me, the foreshadowing of the many unpleasant things my future would hold.

Karen and I are friends on Facebook these days, and on occasion, I talk to her parents. Hopefully, after all these long years, Karen has forgiven me.

***

About the time I hit puberty, the war with my mother escalated. I was very rebellious and we would have raging battles. My mother was still fond of the board but one day there came an end to that. We had a major upset and my mother was chasing me around the house with the board. I ran outside, what would the neighbors think? My mother followed me, but I was a weasely, crafty little person. I had learned to survive. When my mother came out of the house, I ran in and locked all the doors, locking her out. She was understandably fit to be tied, but she didn't chase me around the house with the board ever again.

A truce in our battles eventually came. This was around the time money was tight in our house because my father was on sabbatical working on his PhD. To help make ends meet, my mother went to work. At first, she started as a substitute teacher at the junior high around the corner from our house.

While my mother never was and never would be a militant women's libber, she took to working outside the home like a duck to water. She got a full-time teaching job at the Catholic high school I would eventually attend and she loved it. She was very fulfilled teaching Home Economics, and she liked having her own paycheck. Working satisfied an emotional need and helped with her fear of financial insecurity.

When my father's career got going again, my mother continued to work just because she loved it. Ironically, the only problem she experienced at work was keeping discipline in her classroom which the nuns didn't like. Again there was that divide between the way my mother was at home, and the way she was outside the house.

As it was, when my mother went to work, at home we were no longer constantly inventoried. My mother didn't have time to enforce the rules so closely. We just had to be sure that the kitchen was clean before my mother got home, and if we could do that, we enjoyed a little peace.

***

My drinking and drug use began in Seventh Grade shortly after I abandoned Karen, but at first, it was relatively benign. Seventh, Eighth and Ninth grade passed relatively uneventfully. My grades slipped a bit in Seventh and Eighth grade, but I had a good teacher those years, coincidentally named Sr. Regina. Sr. Regina was a dynamo, red-faced and stout, with a great heart and a talent for nurturing. I only got in real trouble with her once, for cussing at an older nun. Mostly Sr. Regina was supportive and encouraging, and I did well in environments like that. I guess this balanced out the depression I was feeling elsewhere, and I'm sure I'm not the only one who felt like that. Middle school is a bitch for everyone.

I continued with my struggle for second-tier status in my class. I continued my dancing with Tina and Karen W. But I had a double life. What I did a lot of was hanging out with third-tier Veronica, and that involved stealing and drugs and alcohol. We shoplifted a lot. In a way, it was necessary. My mother wouldn't buy me clothes, I could only sew them. That plan was a non-starter in 1971. So we would shoplift and I would come home with clothes. If my mother asked me about the clothes, I told my mother they were hand-me-downs from Veronica. This was ludicrous given that Veronica was a D-cup and I was a vanishing double-A. But my mother bought it. Mom was a little distracted by then because she was working.

Veronica and I also smoked, and we would get alcohol and marijuana whenever we could. Stealing alcohol from parents was common, but you couldn't get carried away with that, or you were sure to get caught. Sometimes an older friend would buy alcohol for us, or we would get a complete stranger to feel sorry for us and buy it. Tony would get us marijuana. It's odd; life just went on like normal with Tony. That was always happening in my life, something bad would happen, and then everything would go back to seemingly normal.

My parents didn't know about any of my extracurricular activities yet. The worst that happened was that once in a while, I would get caught smoking.

By Ninth grade, Veronica went to a public school; she didn't move on to the Catholic school like most of the rest of the class did, but I stayed friends with her. I also stayed friends with Tina. I made a new friend in Ninth Grade. Coincidentally, her name was also Regina.

Regina and I smoked a lot of marijuana. Her brother was nice, and she always had money, and her brother would always be buying marijuana for us. I have visions of rooms of young potheads sitting around giggling. So mostly, this was pretty harmless.

Friend tiers were melting away by Ninth Grade so these classifications became less important. Certainly, Regina was a respectable friend. She came from a wealthy family, she was a relatively good student, she was pretty, and she had boobs. One thing that friendship did do was to improve my standing with Tony, something I still desperately yearned for. In his eyes, Regina was cool, and Tony would spend time with us even though I myself still hadn't made it out of my 'pariah' stage with him. I probably never did until we were grown-ups. But for then, at least, the double life was continuing, the respectable friends on one hand, and the disrespectable, trouble-making friends on the other.

***

The real trouble started in Tenth Grade, the year my sister got married. My self-destructiveness was accelerating. I was a strange mix of anger, rebelliousness, fear and shame, although I could not have told you that. I had no understanding of it myself. So I acted out. Veronica had rowdy friends at the public school, and we would smoke literally anything and sniff glue. That's when I discovered PCP, my drug of choice for all of Tenth Grade. Along with alcohol. Alcohol was big for me by then and me drinking to oblivion was fairly common whether someone else was around or not. In my drug years, my drinking was pretty straightforward – I found kids who believed that getting wasted was the socially acceptable thing to do, and in fact, the desirable outcome. There was no pretense of social drinking and didn't need to be. We wanted to be wasted.

    I had to be wasted. I needed to escape by then as I was highly depressed, I think both from the things that had happened to me and due to biochemical imbalance. At that time, the high from the drugs and alcohol wasn't even the most important thing to me. I needed something beyond the high, I needed the oblivion. Oblivion meant I didn't have to feel. PCP did that for me, it completely distorted reality although not always quite the same way. PCP is an elephant tranquilizer, and is notorious for its variety of effects - acting at times as a stimulant, depressant or hallucinogen - and for its unpredictability. That didn't matter to me. Looking back on it now, I largely remember a sickening feeling when I smoked it, but I needed it, whatever the outcome.

* * *

In Tenth Grade, I had a boyfriend, Terry. He was the high school basketball star. Having a basketball star boyfriend was marvelous, it gave me a feeling of prestige that held back the vast overwhelming and ever-present tide of feeling uncool. I can't say I had any great affection for Terry. I was just trying to fit into the social network successfully.

    On multiple occasions, Terry and I hung out with friends at their houses with apparently little adult supervision. We would drink and get high, and then Terry and I would go into a back bedroom and try to have sex. At that time, the sex itself wasn't important to me and I don't remember feeling any physical desire. Sex was just another requirement for being cool.

    The sexual adventures of Terry and I never ended well, likely drugs and alcohol were making Terry impotent. I of course blamed our lack of success on myself, on my sexual inadequacy and my belief I was physically deformed. This failure was just another confirmation of what I believed after my episode with Tony.

    Still, though all that had happened was some fumbling in the dark, the other people there always gave Terry and I approving grins when we came out of the bedroom. It was supremely cool to 'score.' I myself felt dirty and ashamed, a sickly feeling in my stomach, but it was a price I was willing to pay.

* * *

In these years, I did have one healthy escape – I loved to go to the library and would go any chance I got. Science fiction/fantasy were the ticket for me. I must take after my Uncle Erv, the science fiction writer. I also had one very nice nun in Ninth Grade, Sr. Maria John. She taught Creative Writing. We had fun in her class; she allowed a lot of great debates. This suited me because I was in a semi-polite war with the world even under the best of circumstances. Later in life, I managed to get away from drugs and alcohol. Thankfully, the love of literature is still with me.

By this time, what had become evident was that I needed a job. I needed money for drugs and alcohol, and I needed money for clothes because I really didn't like stealing, truth be told. Besides, I was afraid of getting caught. Veronica was the ringleader on this as well. She got us jobs at the local Dunkin Donuts. We moved on from there and got jobs as waitresses at IHOP. I almost didn't get that job. I smoked PCP on what was supposed to be my first day on the job and was entirely whacked out. The boss lady felt sorry for me. I think she just thought I was nervous. So I did get to go to work and keep that job and then I had money to do with as I willed.

So that was the routine. Work. School, although that was suffering a lot by now. Drugs. Alcohol. Getting totally obliterated on PCP. Getting passed-out drunk. My father put a lock on his liquor cabinet when he found out I was stealing from it, and he stopped drinking beer entirely because he couldn't lock it up. My father, and his one beer a day and an occasional highball, and my mother, a complete teetotaler. I must have gotten the alcoholism from my grandfather, my father's father. Somehow, it had skipped a generation.

Eventually, my drug and alcohol use progressed. There were incidents. My parents discovered the drugs. They became more aware of how often I was drunk. I was staying out until all hours of the night with all kinds of strange people. Often I found myself and my friends riding in cars with men I didn't know to places I didn't know, sometimes even hitchhiking. I was too in a fog to register where we were or how we got there. If I had had to call for help, I wouldn't have been able to tell anyone where I was. I spent many nights in basements with strangers wasted in a PCP haze. I was very, very lucky nothing bad happened to me, like maybe rape or death. It certainly could have happened.

Then something seemingly-catastrophic occurred. My father put his foot down. He said, "No more of these friends for Regina."

So I stopped hanging out with them. All of them. I later often thanked my father in my head, and I still do. But later I also realized I was ready for it. If I had wanted to keep doing drugs, I would have, but I didn't. I didn't need friends to drink though, and the drinking was not something I was going to give up. Thus started my pattern of drinking alone.

With my sister married and her perfection complete, my downfall was well on its way. Tony got married, too, and didn't invite me to the party afterward even though he invited the little sister of his wife. When I heard that, it felt like my heart sunk to my toes. Somehow that still stings me even now when I think about it. I was still not good enough, not cool like Tony and his friends, not fitting in. It was a deep truth that I was still a pariah.

As for Chris, he frowned upon my drinking entirely and wouldn't let his friends talk to me.

As for me, it had always been true that my father never disciplined us. Never. When Dad put his foot down it meant something, and so we all obeyed.

* * *

And that was Drugs and The End of Drugs. More drinking lay ahead for me.

CHAPTER 7

God and Alcohol

Eleventh Grade dawned uneventfully. I was back to being a nerd again. For a while in Ninth and Tenth Grade, I had worn hard contacts lenses but my eyes stopped tolerating them, so I was back to glasses. I had no friends, that is to say, no friends except alcohol. I did have a driver's license and a cooperative liquor store so I could drink outside of the house and not get caught.

Still, when I was at home, I would drink a lot and do my best to hide it. Standard fare was rose wine camouflaged in a plastic Tupperware cup. This I filled from a jug that I hid in the very back of my closet. I would sit in the living room by myself and drink my wine and listen to depressing music on the record player. A particular favorite was Janis Ian; it doesn't get any more depressing than that. But there were also Judy Collins and Joan Baez. The themes of the songs were always lost or unrequited loves. There may or may not have been anyone specific I was thinking about then. Just in general, I believed, as my brother had said, that no one would ever love me.

So there I would sit in that beautiful golden living room. I would drink my wine and listen to all that tragic music. Some day, I would play melodramatic songs on the piano like, "What now my Love, Now that you've left me?" or "Where is Love?"

from *Oliver*, singing at the top of my lungs. As I drank, I would feel the welcome familiar warmth of the alcohol come over me. Most importantly, I would feel like I was not alone. The music was my company in all my desolate loneliness.

My father would pass through the living room on his way upstairs and wonder out loud about why I was attracted to such depressing music. Today, someone may have recognized this as depression and gotten it treated, but back then, no one did things like that. It probably would not have mattered even if my parents had gotten me help. I was nowhere near ready to face the trauma I had buried so deeply inside me. Medication alone can only do so much.

I did attempt suicide somewhere in that period, or just before. The idea came to me after I had started drinking. I'm not sure what prompted my melodramatic despair this particular time, I just wanted the despair to end. I don't think I really wanted to die, somehow the potential outcome of my actions wasn't real to me. In the histrionic way I had when I was drinking, I took a bottle of Darvon and got blind drunk. Mixing pills and alcohol could kill you, right? That had happened to a girl on the news back then. But it didn't kill me. The next morning I was very grateful for that. My parents never knew about this, and life just went on. I shudder now to think of all the truly dangerous things I did in all my life's lost confusion.

* * *

I went to an all-girls Catholic high school. A number of months into my Eleventh Grade year, someone invited me to a religious retreat. To this day I am grateful for that. Despite my drinking, I have many good memories of high school because of it.

There was an organization around this retreat, and it was called Echo, and activities were ongoing for those who were involved in it. I didn't know that at the time, but I went on the retreat anyway. At one point, letters are distributed to those on the retreat from people who had been on one before. I was very touched by the letters. I didn't have any friends and certainly didn't get the most letters, but I got some. In my state of loneliness, that was very moving to me. Then we went on with the rest of the weekend with services and testimonials.

At the end of this retreat, there was something called a 'closing.' It was very, very emotional. Again, people who were part of the program and had been on one of these retreats before showed up for the closing. There were tears and music. There was a very charismatic priest involved called Fr. Jeff. I adored him. He later died of AIDS after reminding me that I was always telling him he was full of it. I don't remember that. But I guess I was always telling the whole world it was full of it in those days, so it's not surprising.

I got very involved in this program. I always had a spiritual longing. After all, I had run away to the sanctuary when I was in Seventh Grade and had a fight with my friend. Up until Echo, I had yet to find anything that fulfilled it in me. This came close.

I made several close friends, Denise, Karlene and Cat. They were really smart girls and had their heads on straight. They had all gone to the same elementary school and had known each other forever, and they took me under their wing. They had been in Sr. Maria John's class in ninth grade with me and observed all my 'debating' while I was at war with the world, and they had always found it very amusing.

Better than friends even, the Echo program had boys! My high school, La Reine, had a brother school named McNamara, and boys went on these retreats, too. Not the same retreats, the retreats weren't co-ed, but the boys did come to closings, and I had a ball.

This started a good track for me. I got involved in a lot of extra-curricular activities. My grades improved. I had fun. I got new 'soft' contacts. I had a life again.

* * *

With all these good things in my pocket, my senior year was amazing for me. I got good grades and graduated in the top five percent of my class when I didn't even know that was a thing. Extracurricular activities included National Honor Society, Class Council, Concert Choir, and more. I was even Editor of the literary journal. I look back on this now and know this was quite a privilege.

We would also have large emotional gatherings for Echo closings, and afterwards, we would sit around with a smaller group of friends who played folk guitar and we would sing. I felt safe and loved. I also got myself a nice high-school boyfriend there, Frank, who was just the cutest thing. Just like Tigger, he had boundless energy and was so much fun.

Later, when I got to AA, I learned that this kind of experience isn't unusual. It was fulfilling that spiritual longing in me, but it wasn't true spirituality. "We mistook high emotionalism for true spiritual feeling," it says somewhere in the AA literature. But it certainly beat the alternative, which was nothing.

By the time high school graduation came around, it seemed I was on top of the world. The future seemed teeming with promise. I got accepted into the Honors program at the state university. My parents, while concerned about some of my behavior, were proud of me.

***

There was definitely cause for my parents to be concerned as my double life continued. I was still drinking, still living a double life. I would drink alone and drive around. I spent a lot of time at the 'library'. Sometimes I actually did go to the library, but most of the time I was drinking. There was a lot of underage drinking at Echo when we got pizza after closings. I don't know why the priests let us get away with it, but they did. Even so, that wasn't enough for me. I would have to drink a six-pack of beer before I went to any of those activities.

My cousin Katherine and I would sit and drink in a parked car on a dead end road that overlooked a hill. There were houses on a bluff behind us and a sloping field of scraggly scrub beneath us. It was the perfect, isolated place to drink without getting into trouble with any grown-ups. Surprisingly, Katherine never judged me for my drinking. This was a relief to me given how I was judged for it at home. While she didn't judge, Katherine never kept up with my drinking either. Even in the best of circumstances, times like these had a way of making me feel like my skin didn't quite fit.

On these forays while I got drunk and Katherine didn't, we would both sit and pontificate on all the world's problems. In the infinite wisdom of high school teenagers, we were sure we had all the answers, the solutions to all the world's ills. Too bad I never could remember the solutions the next day when I woke up with a hangover. I always had terrible hangovers.

I did have high absenteeism in these years, but my grades were good and by then, I was on the good side of the teachers so I got away with it. All in all, between drinking alone, drinking with Echo friends and drinking with Katherine, I was drunk three or four nights a week each week my senior year in high school. I don't mean a little drunk. I mean passing out drunk, usually with throwing up beforehand. Not quite the life one would imagine for a successful high school senior.

There was one incident with my drinking that particularly concerned my parents. It happened that February. I went to see an Echo friend of mine named Sean, he was so handsome and very philosophical, a rampant existentialist. I honestly don't remember what happened. I didn't exactly have black-outs, I had 'brown outs,' so I remember something happened, but I don't remember what.

Whatever it was, it must have scared my parents, because they sent me to my first AA meeting. This involved me going with my perfect older sister, Betsy. As always, the distance of our early years persisted. While Betsy dutifully drove me to the AA meeting and was nice about doing it, there was never any attempt to be close, to try to understand why I was troubled, to offer any counseling or advice. She was not showing care, she was just doing the dutiful thing.

I went to the meeting, but of course, I got very drunk first, you have to do that to go to an AA meeting, don't you? But the people there were all really, really old, and I mean old like over thirty. So I didn't go back, and for whatever reason at that time, my parents just dropped it.

* * *

So that was God and Alcohol, and for a while, it seemed I was getting away with it.

*My high school graduation.
The yellow stole signified membership in the National Honor Society.
I was seemingly on top of the world.*

CHAPTER 8

College Drunk

The summer after high school graduation passed hazily. There were lots of parties, and everyone was still in touch as no one had gone away to school yet. Those post-graduation parties were like a trip to Disney World for me, surrounded by these high school friends, nice people, good students, who were drinking like me.

I remember being at one graduation party at Ocean City, MD. Someone's parents had let us stay at their luxurious beach house. It wasn't quite on the beach but in the near vicinity, and was full of happy beach ambience. At the party, the keg of beer was flowing generously, the girls were funny and lively and matching me drink for drink, the guys were boisterous and amusing. Everyone was dancing with abandon as Bennie and the Jets and other spirited songs blared on the record player. Feeling the music and the laughter and the camaraderie, I felt a warmth come over me. I was one of the gang and fitting right in. At least in that one carefree moment, no one was judging me. These types of moments were rare and precious, but in my heart of hearts, I always knew they would only be a temporary respite.

I was still dating Frank and he was a lot of fun. Energetic, determined, smart. Also a heavy drinker, but he could handle it better than I could. He was going to college planning a double major in economics and some kind of science, and I was going to be in the Honors program and be a physics major. We were both going to the same school and it was within driving distance, so we were going to commute together.

One thing did happen right before we went to school. I went on vacation with Frank and his parents to Nags Head. I don't remember much of that trip, I was too drunk. I do have one fond memory of driving in Frank's car, he took his own instead of riding with his parents. We were going to stop at Busch Garden's on the way down. Cat Steven's *Wild World* was blaring on the radio, and I remember that for a brief moment, I was happy. I still love that song, and to this day, it always reminds me of Frank.

The relationship scared me, in particular with what is the normal young adult exploration of sex. I was terrified about not being good at sex. It was a horrible experience, and for a long while, this feeling was a pattern for me due to what had happened with my brother. So I did the most logical thing. I broke up with Frank.

I'm not sure when I did this, either right before or right after we started school. I wrote Frank a long melodramatic letter about something else entirely as the purported reason we had to break up. I remember watching Frank read it and the expression on his face. He was completely baffled. Poor guy. How could he know what was going on inside me?

We broke up. We got back together again. We broke up, we got back together again. Finally he'd had it, and said that's enough. And we really broke up. This didn't end well for me.

***

In the meantime, I was experiencing culture shock. I had come from this protected, insulated world with a connected community and now I was at Big State U. Life there was completely different. It was also the time the shock hit me that I was no longer the smartest person in the room.

It was too much for me. By then, I wasn't commuting with Frank anymore; I was driving myself. I was at the same university where my sister had been in the sorority, but eight a.m. found me at the liquor store at an off-campus dive, the only place to buy alcohol that was open. My drinking went full bore. I think I missed at least half my classes, and as it turned out, I didn't finish the semester. This was how this happened:

One rainy autumn night, I was driving around drinking as I often did. Crystal Gayle was singing on the radio, "Don't it make my brown eyes blue," and I was singing along as loudly as I could and crying about Frank. Then I had a genius idea. I was the queen of melodrama by then and I decided that I would check myself into a mental hospital. I have no idea why now, but at the time, I thought this was the ideal solution for me.

I drove around looking for a hospital for quite a while. I went to two hospitals. The first one was the ancient, red-brick psychiatric hospital downtown, the monolith where my father had been in after my grandfather committed suicide. Thankfully, the staff wouldn't keep me there, that hospital was infamous for the nightmare stories surrounding it and its patients. The second hospital was the city's dreary, gray general hospital bordering on the ghetto, and the staff there was willing to admit me. So there I was, eighteen years old in the hospital, side by side with their patients hearing voices and doing the Thorazine shuffle. This was my first, but not last, hospitalization.

The next morning when I woke up, I was mortified. What would people think of me? I also knew that I wouldn't have ended up in the hospital if I hadn't been drinking. I knew the drinking had affected my judgment just like it had when I had almost killed myself in another melodramatic moment.

The doctors at the hospital kept me there for a week. There were lots of questions about my situation. There was some thought it might be to do with my drinking. There was some thought that it might have something to do with my parents, but I denied that. There was no real recognition of the depression I was suffering, or maybe there was and they just couldn't treat it then. I certainly didn't know I was depressed. Be it nature or nurture, I was used to it, it seemed normal to me.

So I went home. Even I had decided my drinking was odd by then, so when I got out, I went to an AA meeting. It was a different meeting than the one I had gone to before, and it had young people there. Most importantly, there was a cute guy there, Steve. I probably wouldn't have gone back if there wasn't. But there was, so I did.

I took incompletes in my courses that semester, telling my teachers I had a fatal illness. After all, in AA, didn't people say that about alcoholism? My teachers felt sorry for me.

I never knew what Frank thought of me after that and I remain embarrassed about it, although we are friends on Facebook now and he seems to be over it.

* * *

There was a movement at that time to address alcoholism in young people. There was quite the community of young people in AA. This seemed like a good thing to me. There were lots of activities, and that was helpful.

No surprise, things didn't work out with Steve. In stepped Carl. I needed someone, someone to love me to prove I was lovable. Someone to make me respectable like my sister. So Carl and I dated, and stayed sober, and got engaged. I went back to school, this time in Engineering, and school went reasonably well.

Carl was a really smart guy, and a nice guy, too, but I had a problem. Although life had gotten a little away from this, I still had it ingrained in me. Carl was a second-tier boyfriend. He wasn't the handsomest. Actually, he was very handsome, he was just too tall. That was even his nickname, 'Too Tall Carl.' In hindsight, this seems ridiculous.

Also, I was getting restless. I had managed to stay sober most of a year, but I decided I wanted to drink again. I had heard the term 'situational alcoholic', someone who drinks when their wife dies or they lose their job. I decided that term applied to me, although I'm not sure now how I rationalized that.

At first, the drinking was just a little bit, a beer here and there. But I am a true alcoholic, and that is never, ever going to be enough for me. So it started to be more. And it started to be sneaky because Carl was still staying sober in AA. Then I knew that if I wanted to drink the way I wanted to drink, I would have to break up with Carl.

I still feel badly about this, although Carl and I are also friends on Facebook and he apparently only has good memories. It was some relief to me when I heard this as for a long time, I felt very guilty for hurting him.

Also, given what was going to happen in my marriages later, I often feel sad that I did this. I'm sure my life would have been less of a struggle than it became if I had married Carl instead of the men I did. But, evidently, that was not the journey God had planned for me.

Exit Carl, enter Greg, and I was off to the races. I wouldn't come up for air for another six years.

***

I met Greg at a party with mutual friends. When I met him, Greg was a hippie-ish musician with shoulder-length wavy hair that reminded me of Tony. That drew me to Greg instantly. The first night Greg and I met, we got drunk and had sex. I was more okay with this by then because everything had worked out okay with Carl. So Greg and I met, we got drunk, had wild, passionate, excellent sex, and that was the story of our relationship. Along with high drama. There was a lot of high drama, and that went on off and on for two years.

My drinking took off then. I was still living at home, and nominally going to school. Somehow my parents figured out then that I was having sex, and that was a big problem. That "no pre-marital sex" thing, although the rest of the world had changed in that regard in the 60s.

When my mother found out, she called me an unpaid prostitute and didn't speak to me for a month. I was conflicted by that, but I wasn't giving up Greg or the alcohol. When my father found out, he knocked me across the room, and that's saying something.

So I had to move out.

In the usual contrast to me, my respectable sister and her

husband had their first baby.

***

Greg and I went looking for a room to rent for me off campus, where theoretically, I was still trying to go to school. We found a very nice room in a quaint little house about ten minutes away.

There were four people living there including me. Two lived upstairs with their own upstairs kitchen, and two downstairs with another. I was downstairs, so my primary roommate was the other 'downstairs girl,' Lee Ann. She was a firecracker. A force of nature. She came from a wealthy family with very nice, loving parents and a brother who lived out of town, and she was well-taken care of. She was the life of the party, and she would lead the band of college cohorts dancing around in the living room. Not a classic beauty, but certainly cute, with a shock of Peter Pan hair. She had a great big heart, and still does to this day. We are still friends.

Lee Ann liked to drink. Not drink like me, but certainly a lot. So we were good roommates and we would have animated conversations about feelings and other philosophical stuff while we sat on our couch. Only up to eleven o'clock though. Lee Ann could stop. She would drink and drink, but no matter what, at eleven, she went to bed.

My drinking wasn't like that, it wasn't like that at all, and I don't remember most of it. In fact, much of this period of my life passed in a gray haze full of foggy drunks and foggy, painful, debilitating hangovers. I was always moving between the two, from one kind of fog to another, and then back to fog. This went on for the rest of my college career. All this time, I knew without any shadow of a doubt that I was an alcoholic. I was just powerless to do anything about it, mostly because although I was not actively suicidal, I didn't want to live.

***

By the time I was in college, I had become a daily drinker. I drank every day until I passed out drunk. Every day. I had expanded my tastes to hard liquor. My favorite in the end was vodka – vodka and cranberry juice in the summer, and vodka and kahlua in the winter. That was in addition to, not in place of, all the beer and wine.

While some of my friends were dabbling in other substances, I stayed away from them. Drugs took me from point A, sober, to point B, wasted instantaneously. At this point in my drinking, I loved the progression of getting drunk, that feeling of 'dizzy and delightfulness' that I never got when doing drugs. I liked the in-between, the welcome warmth of the diffusing alcohol, the enjoyment of the ensuing melodrama. I loved playing dramatic music as the evening went on. One day I would be happily bellowing "To life, to life, l'chaim!" The next day I would be back to crying with Janis Ian. This melodramatic state was the cozy in-between for me, the intoxicated feelings that moved me. I didn't like being really out of it so much by the time I was done, slurring my words, not having a coherent thought and just embarrassing myself, but by then it would be too late, I didn't have an off switch.

I still had no compunction about drinking alone. When my friends went out to bars, I didn't go because I could not afford to drink as much at a bar as I needed to. I would stay home and play what someone in AA once called 'Drink and Dial.' I'd get drunk and call up people I knew and drone on incoherently. There was a special kind of sickly shame the morning after those calls. I could always dimly recall those conversations and know I had embarrassed myself.

Still, there was a lot of drinking in college by a lot of people. I had a variety of friends in my social circle who drank to some degree, including college classmates and friends from high school who were at the same university. Without exception, each of those friends went on to a professional career. They became engineers, lawyers, doctors or PhDs. I was always a step behind, struggling in all my classes. I never accomplished as much as any of them, despite how 'smart' I had once thought I was.

We did have some good times, but I never felt completely comfortable with any of them. There were my friends from class who didn't drink. I didn't spend much time at their parties, I always made some excuse to leave. Those people weren't any fun, and it seemed like they were always looking down on me.

There was another group of engineering classmates and high school friends who drank a lot but nowhere near as much as I did. I had to be careful with my drinking around them so they wouldn't question me. But on some occasions, this set of friends would relax and get drunk with me, and I would have a fleeting, precious moment where I felt like I belonged.

Then there was the circle of partiers I lived with who drank and did drugs, still not quite like me but at least their goal to get really high was basically the same. Ironically, of the people I knew, this was the group that came from money. They were always a little more chic than me, so even here I struggled to fit in.

Finally, there were strangers I came in contact with in one way or another. On one scary occasion, there were some people I hooked up with at a dilapidated liquor store that was the only one open on Sunday. Those people looked like low-life criminals but they drank like me, and the list of people who would drink with me was getting shorter and shorter. I brought them home. This is where my life was taking me.

* * *

Some people who are heavy drinkers are functional alcoholics, but by this point I was not. I had trouble with any kind of responsibility. Sometimes I attended classes and sometimes I didn't. Sometimes I dropped a semester and sometimes I didn't. Sometimes I went to work and sometimes I didn't. Long after I got sober, I would have terrifying dreams about waking up at two p.m. with a hangover and realizing I hadn't shown up for work and hadn't called in. Or that I'm in college and I realize I'm signed up for a class that I didn't remember and hadn't shown up to all semester. Or dreams where I had been drinking, which always left me baffled and horrified.

It was the era of DWIs and I got pulled over many times, but I always managed to cook up a believable sad story. I'd be crying and the officers would feel sorry for me and let me go. On one occasion, I even had a car accident. I ran over the back end of a lady's car while I was dead drunk. Funny thing is, when it first happened, I thought, "If I just keep driving, no one will notice." My mind was really telling me that! However, my little green beat-up old-style Volkswagen bug would not cooperate, it was totaled. (A sad demise for such a classic!)

Fortunately, the lady I hit wasn't hurt, and I was really worried about that. Someone at the scene called my mother and told my mother how heroic I was as my one concern as I lay on the sidewalk waiting for the ambulance to come was whether or not the other lady was okay. If that bystander had only knew the truth, that conversation probably would have gone differently.

I broke my nose in this accident, but otherwise, I was fine. When the police came, I talked my way out of it again. I didn't even get a ticket. I'm glad the other lady wasn't hurt. Not sure I would have been able to live with myself otherwise, not that I was doing such a good job of that as it was. The consequences of this accident were nowhere near enough for me to consider not drinking, not continuing my slide into slow suicide.

* * *

Somewhere in there, Greg and I broke up for the final time. I believe I had a nervous breakdown at that point. The ground seemed to come out from under me. Literally. One day, I was carrying a tray at work and dropped it because it seemed the floor had slipped right out from under me. This only served to make my drinking worse. Often, I drank all day long.

When my drinking got this bad, I began to hear well-meaning concern from my friends and teachers. One time, Lee Ann and I and a friend went to Baltimore to visit another one of our friends, Dede. Dede had lived in our off-campus house but had graduated and was going to medical school up there. Dede's parents had put her up in a luxurious, interior-decorated condo we referred to as the Plum Passion Pit.

During that visit, each girl got called on the carpet for something in a considerate way, as was usual for us. When it got to be my turn, I got called on the carpet for my drinking. I always found that ironic given that they were at that moment drinking and doing drugs themselves. But I was the one where people said, "If I ever get as bad as Regina, I'll do something about my drinking."

Another time I had a grade on a test that I went to talk to the teacher about and he somewhat scolded me. "If you ever came to class, you'd be doing better." I was insulted. I went to his class at least fifty percent of the time, which was twice as much as I went to any other class.

Once, I had an eight o'clock class that I obviously had trouble getting to. But one day, I got up, took a shower and brushed my teeth like a normal person, put on clean clothes, and went to class. As I was standing outside of class with some other students, one asked, "Regina, have you been drinking already this morning?" I hadn't. The alcohol was still oozing out of my pores from the night before.

During this period, I had become estranged from my family entirely, and it was my fault. I just didn't show up to anything anymore, and none of them came looking for me. I didn't even show up to Christmas dinner until it was over because I had a bad hangover and was sick all day. My Aunt Bobby later told me my mother had been very sad about that.

Even my father stepped away from me. At one point when I was complaining to him about something my mother had done, he looked at me gesturing for me to stop. "Peace," he said, which left me feeling wholly deflated and confused. My longtime ally against my mother had rejected me.

I did call my father one day. I had smoked some marijuana on top of the alcohol on this day for some reason. I remember calling my father, I remember talking to him, but I don't remember what I said. Probably some fairly angsty thing about some kind of cosmic loneliness. My poor father, how heartrending that must have been to hear.

After that, my father called every week for a while and begged me to go see a psychiatrist. He said he would pay for it. He literally begged me. He said something then that I didn't understand then and maybe never will. He said, "Regina, you're just like me." But he wasn't an alcoholic, so I couldn't see it and I still don't to this day. Still, something in him connected deeply with me. When he would call me like this, I would just tell him I was fine, there was nothing to worry about so he didn't have to call me. That was the last year he was alive.

The feelings were the worst. The shame on top of shame on top of shame. I had started out broken, and I had broken all The Rules. I was failing at school. I wasn't a virgin. I was ignoring my family. I was roaring drunk literally all the time. Even taking the trash out was shameful. The whole neighborhood could hear the rattling because the only things in the trash bag were beer cans.

I'm sure at some point, you have all known some pitiful creature like I was at that time, the person who comes into the bar with obvious problems that everyone avoids. My AA sponsor says it best. "I was a sorry drunk. People were sorry when they saw me coming."

Shame will keep you drunk. I'd drink because I was ashamed, I'd vow I wouldn't drink the next day, but then I would. I had to. It was the only thing that dulled the pain of the shame. Then I was even more ashamed.

Occasionally, I would try out an AA meeting, but I just couldn't seem to feel connected. There's a saying in AA that goes something like, "For me, to drink is to die." I'm here to tell you, if you don't care if you die, that saying is meaningless.

* * *

So there I was, the College Drunk. There was no hope for me. There was no more double life for me. I was only one thing, and that one thing was a drunk.

*Carl and I at an AA dance.
Unfortunately, I wanted to drink more than I wanted Carl.*

Greg and I on our way to a function at school

*My college roommate, Lee Ann.
Lee Ann could drink, but she didn't drink like me.*

*On occasion, my engineering classmates would drink with me.
This picture reflects a rare genuine fun moment.*

With an acquaintance at a Halloween party.
I look happy here, but I was anything but.
It was an off-again phase with Greg.
I had gone to a bar the night before and spent the night with a stranger I met there.
I was sick as a dog with a hangover until I started drinking again,
And I was failing out of all my classes.
Appearances can be deceiving.

Baltimore Inner Harbor with some friends (I am second from the right)
Again, I was miserable and hungover from the night before.
I always felt out of step with the others, always one step behind.
Hence, I always felt alone even when I wasn't.

CHAPTER 9

A Prayer and Sobriety

Somewhere in the middle of the fog after Greg and I had broken up, I met another man whose name was Keith. He didn't like my drinking, but evidently, he was a glutton for punishment. I continued to sort of half go to school. I was twenty-three years old by then, going to school on the 'long plan' due to all my bad semesters. Then something happened that would radically change my life.

While I was dating Keith, my father got sick. The day before, my father had seemed perfectly healthy, but then his stomach swelled up. His best friend teased him that he was getting fat, which made my father angry. Then my father went to the doctor. I suppose he and my mother picked someone out of the phone book because my father had never been sick and never went to the doctor. It later turned out that this doctor was not a very good doctor.

Immediately, the doctor put my father in the hospital. It was the same dreary city hospital I had been in when I checked myself into the psych ward when I was eighteen, somehow smelling simultaneously of dust and sterile antiseptic.

Not much long after, we got the word that my father had cancer. I was living in my off-campus house when my mother called me to tell me about it, and as soon as she gave me the news, tears welled in my eyes. My roommate tried to cheer my up. A lot of people get cancer, right? They get treatment and then they get better. But somehow, I knew. I knew this was likely a death sentence, even though I was only twenty-three and not ready to bury my father.

My father was in the hospital for a mere twenty-six days. Those days passed for me in a blur of grief and alcoholic haze. At some point, for some reason we could never figure out as nothing my father had was contagious, the doctors decided to put him in isolation. This meant he had a room of his own, a luxury, but it also meant we had to don drab, yellow, crinkly paper gowns and face masks to go see him. When my father got delirious towards the end, he acted afraid of us which we couldn't understand. But then we thought, maybe he couldn't tell who we were, which left us all in anguish.

My mother went and sat by my father's side and said rosaries during those hospital days. I imagine that the soothing rhythm of my mother's susurrant prayers was a comfort to my father. My father stopped talking entirely after a bit, which was so unusual for him. The last odd thing I remember him talking about happened during the first week he was in the hospital. He was mad about a heavyweight fight where one of the fighters was killed. My father insisted the ref should have stopped the fight. As I recollect it, that's the last thing I ever heard my father say.

My father's behavior during this time confused me. I could only think about how my father had always been such an Easter person. One night, after we knew my father had very little time to live, I told him, "Dad, when you get to that Heaven you're always talking about, you will find out all the answers to life's mysteries, and you will be happy. Please take care of us." My father never answered me, and in his delirium, I don't think he understood me. I was always a little disappointed in that. I guess I always imagined that when his time came, my father would be joyful to go to that marvelous place he called Heaven.

At the end, my father was delirious because his liver

and kidneys had failed him. His body's poisons were coursing through his veins, with his skin and eyes turning yellow from jaundice. My mother got very mad at the hospital because she wanted my dad to have pain medicine and all the staff would give him, even in his very last days, was a couple of Tylenol. My mother, always anti-drugs of all kinds, railed again and again at the nurses. My mom thought that they should have given my dad heroin.

The day my father died, the whole family was at the hospital including my Aunt Bobby. The doctor came and made us wait down the hall while the doctor went into my father's room. As we stood in the waiting room with the harsh December sunlight glaring in the window, I could hear my dad give a loud shout, and then it was over.

Just like that, Daddy was gone.

In a moment like that, things don't seem real to you. I left the hospital alone in a daze. I left my family. I had to. I had to go home alone to drink my pain away. I couldn't drink around my family.

* * *

My whole family took my father's death hard, including my mother. As for my siblings, we never really talked about it. While we were always pleasant and friendly to each other, we rarely ever talked about anything important. Our lives continued the divides forged in our childhoods. When the best way to get yourself out of trouble when you were a child was to get a sibling in worse trouble, or if one is perfect like Betsy, familial bonds are forever altered.

Personally, I wasn't ready for my father's death in any way. Even though my alcoholism had created a distance, I was lost without him. Still, for a year after he died, I was also really mad at him. My father had been my champion, and sometimes my only friend, and he had left me.

To this day, I feel at least partially responsible for my father's death. People can decide to die, in a way, when they are very heartbroken, and then their bodies naturally obey. I know my father was literally brokenhearted about me. I wasn't his only heartbreak at the end of his life, but I was certainly one of them. I don't feel bad about this now that I am sober. I know sobriety is what my father would have wanted for me, and I am sure he is very happy wherever he may be.

* * *

When my father died, I did the only thing I could do, I drank more, if such a thing is possible. Despite this, my boyfriend, Keith, wanted to marry me. I didn't really want to marry him. At that point, I was much more interested in drinking. I was beyond even the call of the need to be married.

I had moved home to my mother's house after my father died, and then moved to a friend's as my war with my mother continued. This friend was a classmate named Joe. Joe had graduated from college already and had a good job and went out to work every day. I would sit and drink alone on his couch after he went to bed. My life was in shambles. I had all the same old problems. My drinking was terrible. I was failing at school again. Keith and I were barely seeing each other. I had few friends left who would have anything to do with me.

One night as I was sitting there in my misery, something came to me and I said a simple prayer. It was to my father. I said, "Dad, I don't want to live like this anymore." I believe what happened to me next was an answer to that prayer, although it took some time for the end result to come to fruition.

What happened next was that I got pregnant. The baby was Keith's.

* * *

Getting pregnant changed my whole reality. I never had been exceedingly careful with birth control. I still had that thought that my parts weren't put together right in some way because of what happened with my brother. It's a wonder I didn't get pregnant before this. But this event was completely miraculous to me. I WAS HAVING A BABY! One of the things I had thought would never happen to me, and one that I had dearly desired.

Ironically, Keith did not want to marry me anymore. But

that didn't matter, I was going to have a baby! And so, I became in my mother's terminology, an 'unwed mother'. Very scandalous in those days. As was fitting for a Firstborn Child, my sister was having her own second child, and she was doing it the 'right' way. But for me, nothing could take away the happiness of having that baby.

Naturally, my mother was angry when I achieved my status of unwed mother. Funny story – she was working on her Masters at that time and her thesis was on unwed mothers. I guess she wanted to understand what had happened to me. In one of her courses she read that girls who are close to their mothers are less likely to end up in a situation like this. My mother said, "See, I told you that you should have been closer to me." That makes me giggle even today when I think about it. Even I could see that her interpretation was ridiculously silly, and generally, I wasn't very good about interpreting the things my mother would say.

* * *

I wish I could say I stopped drinking when I got pregnant, but I didn't. I did drastically cut down on my intake though. I saw a Spring morning again, which I hadn't seen in years. Life was beginning to have meaning again for me. I was coming back from the ledge of mindless oblivion.

Eventually, Dominic arrived, as babies do. He became my sun and moon and stars, and practically my reason for living. Although my mother wasn't happy when she found out I was pregnant, she was happy when Dominic was born. She always did love babies.

I just left college when I got pregnant. Once I had the baby, I got a job, and then I went back to drinking. I returned to my high school pattern of being drunk three or four times a week. There were incidents. One time my roommate had to come and get the baby because I was too passed out to feed him. One time I left Dominic home when I went out to get beer, and when I got home, I found I had locked myself out with the baby inside crying.

In addition to these incidents, I started to get miserable again. Then I had a moment of truth. I knew that if I kept drinking, I was going to go back to that oblivion where I had been before. At that moment, I felt in my heart of hearts that if I did that, went back to drinking like that, I would never make it back from the alcoholic ledge again for the rest of my life.

It was a 'now or never' moment. I made a decision in that moment, the most important decision I've ever made in my life.

I decided I wanted to live. That was a gift, my first moment of profound Grace.

It also meant quitting drinking.

But I wasn't going back to AA. Nope, I had done that already. So I went to counseling instead. When I called the counseling agency, I believe I was given an intuitive sense by a God I didn't believe in anymore that I shouldn't say my problem was drinking. Not that I didn't want to quit drinking, I did. But while my conscious mind was not at all aware of it, my unconscious mind was telling me, "You have more things you need to take care of besides the drinking."

It was time to take care of the secrets.

* * *

So there I sat in a counselor's office, twenty-five years old. John was the counselor's name. There, finally the big secret came out of me. The one about my brother. I remember I was crying, sobbing uncontrollably.

Then John asked me what I thought was a really weird question. He asked me, "What are you thinking?" At that moment, I stepped outside of myself and I heard a child in my head saying, "If Daddy were here, everything would be alright. If Daddy were here, everything would be alright." It became clear to me then that this was the voice of a child who had been a victim, and that victim was me.

All the things I had been blaming myself for, all the shame I had carried for years and years, no longer were valid. In fact, I realized that I was a textbook case of the things that people do who had the experiences I had as a child. I had gotten broken and blamed myself.

Thanks to the courage and honesty I finally found in counseling, I was able to do the most important thing of all that I could do in order to get rid of the shame. I was able to forgive myself. This was an imperative to quit drinking, and it was a profound rewriting of my life. This gave me a solid foundation for living that I had never had before.

* * *

I did go home and tell my mother about what had happened with Tony. I had moved back home with Dominic by then. I was always moving back and forth somewhere. My mother's first response was not, "How could your brother do that to you?" She said, "None of my brothers would ever have done that to me." She didn't seem to be angry at Tony about it. In a sense, she was blaming me. I didn't even recognize this but my therapist did, and he was very skillful in addressing it with me.

Besides that negative reaction, it turns out my mother had other stories to tell. Evidently, both my brother and I had been molested by a neighbor, me when I was one and a half, Tony would have been four. I don't remember that, but then a lot of other things related to sex in my childhood began to make sense to me. I won't go into the details, but there were other incidents that had happened in my childhood that my mother had deeply shamed me for, and now I began to understand why. I think it even explains a bit about what Tony did. Something like that twists you as a child.

Of course, per my mother, no one ever did anything about sexual abuse in those days so nothing was done to deal with the neighbor. But I somehow know that even as a child, in my mother's eyes, she blamed me for it.

* * *

John and I obviously had another topic to take care of in counseling, and that was my mother. I didn't go into a lot of the details of my childhood, but John had the sense to understand what was happening based on my mother's behavior at that time. A few months had gone by, and I had moved out of my mother's house by then. Then John gave me the most profound advice I have ever heard in my life. He said,

"Regina, you have to realize that your mother lives on the planet Jupiter. Sometimes you are going to go over there and she will spit in your face and slam the door. You just have to turn around and go back on a better day because you are not the kind of person who can walk away from your mother."

KAZOWIE!

Now I had a way to deal with my mother. I could stop letting her push my buttons, and I could still love her without letting her hurt me. This is advice I never, ever forgot, and many, many times, I had to do exactly what John said. This single thing alone eventually allowed me to have a happy relationship with my mother that lasted even until the day she died.

* * *

Around the time I got sober, my sister and I had a big fight. I was living at my mother's house with my baby son and my sister was there with her children. My oldest nephew wanted me to take him to the playground and I wanted to go. Unsurprisingly I suppose, my mother pronounced that I would not be able to take my nephew as I would never get the housework done that she was expecting of me. I was twenty-five years old, still a slave to my mother's demands. On the other hand, I was becoming more emotionally independent by then and I wasn't willing to be disrespected that way in front of the children. When I said something to my sister about this, her response was, "I have always found our mother to be infinitely wise."

Wow. Just. Wow. I was dumbfounded, although I guess I should not have been surprised. But I thought, "What about all the things that have happened?" I started listing events of our childhood out for Betsy and we eventually got in a huge fight about it. The fight was so dramatic that it ended with actual hair-pulling and throwing things.

Afterwards, to calm down, I bought a six-pack of beer and drove all the way around the DC beltway. This was the second to the last time I ever drank. When I got home, my mother and my sister were calm. They had put their heads together and decided that I had "made all this stuff up in order to keep my father's memory to myself." They really said that. Again I was dumbfounded. Again, my reaction was "Wow."

This point of view of theirs finally freed me. For so many years, I had tried to fit my life, my perspective, in with theirs, and in that process, all I became was the crazy drunk one. When I heard these denials from them, I knew I would never fit my life together with theirs but not for the reasons anyone previously thought. The freedom finally came from knowing we would never fit not because I was out of touch with reality, but because they were.

* * *

It was an enormous relief to me to have a way to deal with my mother in the present on a daily basis. However, that was not the sum total of the work I had to do. By this time, I had blamed my mother for my problems my entire life, and one would argue, justifiably so. In a way, this anger probably saved me, it was reflective of some inner strength, some inner will to survive despite what was going on around me.

Still, what I realized when I decided to quit drinking was that no one was ever going to rewrite history for me. No one was ever going to come back and say they were sorry. Even if my mother had said she was sorry, it would have done little to undo the damage that had been done. The messages were so ingrained in me, the sub-conscious thought that I would never be good enough was too deeply embedded in me for a simple sorry to take it away.

But blaming my mother had to come to an end; it was keeping me stuck. What I clearly understood when I decided to quit drinking was now that I was grown, the quality of my life was dependent on my own decisions. I had been the one choosing to drink, not my mother, and I was the only one who could make the decision for me to not drink. I could drink for the rest of my life and blame her the whole time, or I could make a different choice and have a life. Fortunately, and I am one of the lucky ones, I chose to have a life.

Through counseling and the spiritual awareness that came to me when I quit drinking, I came to realize that my mother did the very best she could with what she had. Instead of blaming, I started forgiving. I never felt a need to confront my mother and ask for an apology as some people do. Despite all my mother's demands, I have always had an intuitive sense that underneath her surface was a great fragility. If she really understood the damage she had done, it might break her. It seems paradoxical, I know, but I also know that it's true. Just like she always loved babies, although probably no one should have ever entrusted them to her.

* * *

I had still been drinking a little over my first number of months with the counselor. At first, I didn't tell my counselor about my drinking, we had other things to talk about. Then, after some of the other stuff was out of the way, I started letting little hints slip. I wasn't going to come out with the whole of it. John was very perceptive though, and then he made another statement I will never forget. John said,

"Regina, you are never going to have the kind of life you could have unless you stop drinking." Bells went off all over my head! Not 'you're a terrible person,' not 'you're ruining your life,' not any of the things I had ever heard before. Just so simple. "You will never have the kind of life you could have…" This made me very hopeful.

Then he said something that really pissed me off. He said,

"And I can't help you with that; you need to go back to AA."

Wait, what? Why couldn't he help me? I had already tried AA, it didn't work! I didn't want to sit around with those people and do nothing but drink coffee and smoke cigarettes (everybody did back then). They were always talking about things like the 12 Steps of AA. I just didn't want to do it.

But I didn't want to drink more than I didn't want to go to AA, and so I went back. It was sort of a tortuous journey. At first,

I avoided any meetings I had gone to before. I'm not sure why. I didn't really have a conscious thought that the people at those meetings would judge me, so I can't explain it. Instead, I went to different meetings in an area close by and went for a few weeks without drinking.

Then came that hair-pulling fight with my sister when I drank a six pack of beer. That night, I went to one of those new AA meetings. A lady there was pretty mean about me drinking. She said, "Regina, maybe you haven't drank enough." I was angry when she said that, but really, I'm glad she did. When she said that, I looked in my soul and knew beyond any shadow of a doubt that I had. I'd had enough; I wanted to live. After that, I only drank one more time, a mere half bottle of wine, which I consumed while I fantasized about how to murder my mother.

Since the bridge at those new meetings was basically burned, I next went back to meetings where I had known people before. As soon as I went to one of my old meetings, I ran into a gentleman, Willy, whom I had been good friends with in my earlier AA days. When Willy ran up and hugged me and welcomed me back and was so excited to see me, I knew that I was finally Home. I was with people like me, people who loved me, people who understood me. I was in a place where I Belonged. All my life, I had ached to feel like I belonged, and finally, there I was. I have not taken a drink since that day, November 4th, 1985.

* * *

You probably have some image of AA meetings from shows on TV. Dreary people sitting in dreary rooms talking about dreary things. AA is not like that, it is not like that at all. In fact, what would strike you most as you approach a room full of recovering alcoholics is the abundant raucous laughter. It's a gallows humor borne of shared suffering, but rampantly funny just the same.

Laughing at ourselves and our foibles, both drunk and sober, is healing. It puts things in a proper perspective. Nothing any of us could have done would be cataclysmic enough to bring the world to an end. Someone else has done the same things I did, or even worse, and lived to tell the tale. This is the nature of fellowship which is a core element of recovery.

There are other aspects that are important in AA. One of them is the 12 Steps. Alcoholism has a physical component, but it is inherently also a disease of feelings. The 12 Steps of AA gave me a way to deal with my feelings, a skill I had never learned as I drowned them all in alcohol instead. The Steps are a very practical instruction book, one I had been missing my entire life.

Another healing aspect of AA comes from working with other alcoholics who are trying to get sober. The journey is often rocky and often the failures outweigh the successes but the successes are worth it. The sense of fulfillment that comes from being able to help someone else who is suffering is profound.

Probably the most important aspect of AA is the spiritual connection of the program. Recovering alcoholics are far from perfect. We are human and subject to the same human pitfalls. But there is something that happens in a one hour AA meeting that is Greater Than The Sum Of All Our Parts. A Power that keeps us sane. I'm sure some people find this in church, but I wasn't able to find it there. Theology isn't practical when it comes to feelings, and church is mostly very serious. There's a saying that goes something like this: "Church is full of people afraid of going to Hell. The basements of churches (where AA's often meet) are full of people who have already been there."

* * *

A funny thing was true for me when I was drinking, probably even all the way back to the time I was fourteen. By then, it was already quite clear that there was something wrong with me. Priest and teachers, or friends and acquaintances, those dabbling in pseudo-psychology, all saw it. It was pretty obvious, even to me. Often people would tell me, "Regina, we know what's wrong with you; you suffer from Low Self-Esteem." They would always appear very pleased with themselves for having diagnosed such an obvious problem. Then off they would go, probably telling me to pray about it. But at least to me, it seemed no one ever told me how to get that precious Self-Esteem.

I always find this amusing now, what good is it to tell

someone they need self-esteem and just leave? Praying about it never worked for me, although I can say that many times, I sincerely tried that.

Then I learned something in counseling. When I took responsibility for my life and stopped blaming my mother, and when I started getting honest about the things that had happened to me, I had a new feeling for me. I felt good about me. I stopped feeling ashamed. I found some dignity, a precious commodity that alcohol had taken away from me. I found some Self-Esteem.

Self-esteem is as simple as that. Tell the truth about how you feel, and take responsibility for your life instead of blaming other people. Praying doesn't hurt either, I found out after all, but it has to be based on practical action. The practical action isn't mystical, it's just a choice, just like choosing to quit drinking. I am happy to say that as much as I have sometimes wandered, those two actions I have been able to get right, honesty and responsibility. Sometimes, they have been the only things I did right. Thankfully for me, it's been enough.

* * *

And that was a Prayer and Sobriety. Not to mention a beautiful baby who is still my sun, and my moon, and my stars.

Little did I know that it would be another nineteen long years before I was in complete recovery. Remaining still were grave emotional disorders that I wasn't even aware of. I still had a thing about men.

Keith and I in front of his parent's house when he still wanted to marry me. I was much more interested in drinking than in marrying him.

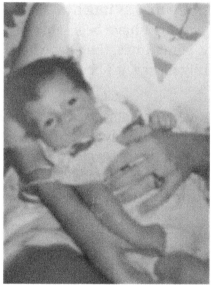

My newborn baby, Dominic, born with a full head of hair

CHAPTER 10

The Happy Family

Yes, if it isn't obvious by now, I have a Man Thing. You may ask what that is. Some people would call it co-dependency, but that's just another label to me. I'm already labeled alcoholic and mentally ill, why would I need another label? I have been codependent with my children for sure. I have enabled men I was involved with, also for sure. But I just like to call it a Man Thing. (Not to be confused with anyone's private parts!)

Nor is it surprising that I would have a Man Thing. Any woman who believes no one will ever love her will always need some semblance of a love, no matter how flawed.

For many years I set my sights on handsome, unattainable men like Tony. Greg had been the worst of these. I was trying to rewrite the vast rejection of what was for me essentially my first love, trying to rewrite the messages Tony gave me. Finding someone like Tony and having them love me would undo what he'd done, right? It would prove that what Tony said wasn't true, that I wasn't fractured and fatally flawed. I think that's the way our subconscious always sees this, and so we repeat the pattern, again and again trying to rewrite the past. This caused me no end of heartache when I was a teenager and young adult, leading to one ill-fated infatuation after another until my alcoholism took me past the point of even caring.

When I got some dignity back in my life because I got sober, I was generally attracted to men who were like my father, brilliant and entertaining, ones who would sweep me off my feet and make me feel like a queen. Certainly, that was especially true with both my husbands. The VIP treatment made me feel secure in the relationship whether I was in reality or not. There was a catch to my attraction to these charismatic men. In the midst of the glorious sweep off my feet, I never took the time to look at anything else. I never saw, or even tried to see, what was around and between and behind that, what those men were really like. I never took the time, too busy bathing in the emerald glow of the waves birthed in that romantic whirlwind, too busy reveling in the high of being a queen.

I knew I had issues with men due to my insecurities, but I always forged ahead anyway. My friend, Diane, would say, "You lays your bets, you takes your chances." After one failed relationship or another, she would have a little giggle and say, "I'm not responsible for anyone's poor relationship choices." Then she would help me clean up the mess. On a more serious note, she would repeat this saying to me: "My soul chose this journey. There's something on this path that my soul wants to learn." I'm sure my soul was trying to learn I was lovable, to finally, finally feel like I was good enough. My soul just chose a backwards way of doing it.

This may seem frivolous compared to some of my other problems, but I can assure you that it is very serious. It has caused me just as much pain in my life as alcohol, maybe even more, and has been just as deadly. I wasn't really in recovery until I got over this, and that was a very long time coming.

***

I met Dave when I was a month sober. Dave was big, an ex-college football linebacker, six feet, four with a muscular build. He had black hair and a square face, and he wore appealing expensive men's cologne. For some reason, I guess because of his size, I always felt safe standing next to Dave. He was always very protective of me, at least in the beginning.

Legend has it that when Dave first saw me, he told a friend that I was the one he was going to marry. I think it's because I reminded him of his favorite sister. Whatever the reason, he pursued me relentlessly, so what was I supposed to do?

I didn't take instruction well either, or even well-meaning (and true!) advice. You're not supposed to make any major changes in your first year of sobriety or get in a relationship if you're not already in one. I figured if people could be in relationships they started while they were still drinking, why couldn't I start one sober? Certainly couldn't be any worse, could it? Also, I was an unwed mother, I wanted to be married. So I did get into a relationship, but I'm here to tell you, I don't recommend it. Go ahead and do it, but don't drink over it when the shit hits the fan. Fortunately, I did manage to avoid drinking, at least.

Dave and I dated for three months and then we got married. This is another no-no, know your partner better when you marry them. At first things were fine. Dave was wonderful. He was funny, smart as a whip, conspiratorially irreverent with me, a good dancer, and very caring. One time early on, I came home from work to find a surprise. He had gone shopping for clothes for me and had hung them decoratively all around our room. It looked just like a showroom. For me, who had had nothing growing up and had had to steal clothes, I found this pleasantly overwhelming.

Most of all, Dave reminded me of my father. He even had some of the same obscure books my father had had. I think I was always looking for a man like my father, how could I not? So entertaining, and such a great joy in life. What I found was that the men who came into my life who were like my father unfortunately had some kind of personality disorder of one kind or another. I don't know how my father avoided that. In my family, that was my mother. Some people say that man or woman, we all marry our mothers, and as it turns out, I did.

Dave early on was fully prepared to take on the responsibility of a wife with a child even though I later found out that Dave had a deep fear of financial insecurity. He adopted Dominic. I myself was still grossly underemployed. This was due to my insecurities of basically failing out of college as a direct result of my drinking. Financially, things were never good. Certainly that was an ill contributor to our later problems.

What I did not know, and I certainly did not understand the depths of this, was that Dave was not prepared to have another baby, at least not right at that moment. I wanted one. I didn't admit this to anyone, least of all to myself. But deep in my heart of hearts, I did. I wanted another perfect baby like Dominic, ironically like my mother had wanted another perfect baby like Betsy when she tried to have me. I wanted the white picket fence, I wanted to be happily married, and I wanted to stay home and take care of my perfect, loving little children. So Dave and I went on the 'rhythm method' of birth control. To this day, I don't know why Dave ever agreed to this but he did. Surprisingly, or not as the case may be, I got pregnant. By then, I was only seven months sober, another no-no major change in one's first year of sobriety.

So much for my fears of not being able to get pregnant! I never had the problems my sister and my mother had getting pregnant or having any miscarriages. I don't know why, but I was the opposite. I could get pregnant seemingly at the drop of the hat, which was later proven by a third pregnancy caused by one unprotected moment.

So Dave and I had a baby. My sister and I were again pregnant at the same time, only this time, I was doing it right. I was married.

While Dave hadn't been prepared to have another baby, when he came, Dave was deliriously happy. I had vowed not to have a Jr., but while we were in the hospital, I accidentally called the baby Dave, and then I was stuck. The beaming on Big Dave's face was something I could not refuse.

Little Davey was not like Dominic. He came out crying, and he kept crying for another nine months. Even in the hospital, when Dave and Dave's father went to the hospital nursery, we became aware of this. They stood admiring one of the bundles of awesome joy they saw there only to find out that baby wasn't ours. Ours was the one who was crying. And crying and crying.

Still, we brought the baby home, of course, and Dominic was mostly happy about a baby brother, and sometimes Little Dave was happy, and we all had fun. Sometimes it was difficult. I couldn't leave home to go to an AA meeting without feeling guilty. I would call home while I was out and hear the baby crying and the confusion in Big Dave's voice, who didn't understand, and didn't know what to do about it.

Shortly after Little Dave was born, we bought a little townhouse. We still didn't have a lot of money, and certainly it wasn't like my sister's house. But it was a comfortable house for four of us, with three bedrooms in a neighborhood with a pool and other amenities. The house was at the end of a row of townhouses. The townhouse only had a kitchen window and a sliding glass door in the back so it was rather dark inside, but I loved the coolness of it when I would bring the kids home from the pool, all smelling of chlorine.

Eventually, I met Dave's family. I had already met Dave's father, Sam. Dave had lived with his father and taken care of him before we were married. I had already met his favorite sister, Liz, the one I reminded him of. The family I hadn't met included his mother, Shirley, and his Cinderella-step-sister-like other two sisters. There were four children in that family, Angie the oldest, Dave, the second, then Donna, then the littlest sister, Liz. When Dave's mother found out Big Dave got married, her only response was, "Is she black?" I have no idea why she would ask that.

I was later to find out how bad Dave's family was, actually from one of the evil sisters, Angie. During the time we enjoyed some temporarily-improved relationships with Angie, she told me a story. She told me that when they were growing up, their parents had had problems of their own - major ones. This led to their eventual divorce. Shirley was very depressed when her kids were growing up and had an addiction to Valium. This was common in those days, Valium was Mother's little helper.

Although he loved his children, Sam was kind of clueless about parenting in the sometimes typical helpless man way, and he had a difficult wife, so he was none too cheery. Angie said, "Dave got the worst of it." Liz said their mother paid them no attention and would leave the room when they came in, and their father only paid them negative attention.

Angie was right, Dave definitely got the worst of all of it. He was the only son. His father did not believe in hitting women so he didn't hit the girls, but he had no compunctions about hitting Dave. Funny, when their father had a breakdown later in life over the divorce, Dave was the one who took care of him.

But in Dave's early years, it was a matter of survival. Dave told me he learned to time his dash into the house when he came home so that he could duck under his father's fist. The fist was always, always there even if there was no reason. This continued until Dave was fifteen when he finally stood up to his father.

Unlike mine, Dave's family was not financial stable at any time. His father was a bricklayer and work wasn't always steady. They were always moving to keep one step ahead of eviction. One time, Dave came home from a camping trip with friends to find no one was home at his house. Not only was Dave's family not at home, nothing was there. The family had moved while he was gone and either hadn't told him, or he didn't register it. My guess is the former. Dave sat there for hours in total abandonment, lost and devastated. His father had forgotten to pick Dave up. Fortunately, eventually his father did, but it was too late. The damage was done.

Needless to say, Dave had a lot of problems in school. I didn't find this out until we had been married for five years, but Dave was in a class for the emotionally disturbed in either First or Third Grade, I don't remember which. Either way, it happened when he was pretty young. He had thrown a desk at a teacher, and he had tried to throw another student out a third-story window.

This was the man I married. This is who you marry when you have a problem with men, and you only know someone three months before you marry them.

* * *

The first sign of real trouble was what I like to refer to as the Burger King incident. Dom was about four, and Little Dave was about one. We went to a drive-through at Burger King. For some unknown reason, Big Dave decided to get into a shouting match with the attendant at the window. Over absolutely nothing. It was so bad that I felt I had to get out of there, so I grabbed Little Dave out of his car seat in the back - he was the only one I could get to - and I walked away. It wasn't the last time I walked away with the kids. Eventually, Dave came and found me and persuaded me to come home.

The second sign of trouble was Dave's work thing. When we got married, Dave was working as a car salesman and the market was good so he was making a lot of money. Then the bottom fell out, and Dave's depression fell in. This type of thing went on for a number of years with odd forays into other fields. I'd have to give Dave pep talks to get up and get to work, and I did everything around the house. I was working myself but not making much money. There was the fear of financial insecurity fulfilled.

* * *

Still, life went on, as was my usual way, and we had some very good times with the kids. A third child arrived four and a half years after Little Dave was born, Patrick, and then I got what I always wanted. I got to stay home with the kids. It was arranged in a way by God that I could collect unemployment insurance while I did it for a while, and then we managed somehow, mostly with financial help from my mother. I felt guilty about taking money from my mother, but at the time, I also figured she owed me.

I was home with the kids for two and a half years. That period was one of the happiest times of my life. We did so many fun things, and we made friends with a neighbor, Tina, who had two daughters about the same ages as my kids. I was very active at the kids' school, and their school was simply marvelous in the approach they took. They were cultivating the children instead of the children's test scores. We also went to Cub Scouts and we went to CCD (religious education) at church. We played with the cousins on both sides, most of whom were about the same age.

In the summer, we would have 'Mama school' where I taught the kids with Hooked on Phonics and Hooked on Math. We did science experiments. I told them little stories I had invented about baby elephants that came into our yard. We went to the pool, we ran races and rode bikes, we sang and played piano, we had Christmas sing-alongs with the neighbors, had fabulous birthday parties for the kids, and did something for every occasion. Somehow, we managed all of this in spite of Big Dave.

Not gonna lie – the kids were a handful by the time they had gotten a little older. My kids were all beautiful children. I suppose every mother would say that, but mine really were with their smooth skin and big eyes. Patrick and David looked quite a bit like each other, and they had matching bowl haircuts. Dominic looked more like his biological father, who was half-Asian.

Still, they were challenging. One time after the first grade teacher had had two of my kids, he said, "Mrs. B, you certainly have your hands full." What he didn't know was that the third one was as hyper the two first ones put together. But they were good kids, they were never bad. They were just very curious, and very energetic. I never knew what would happen. I could be drinking a cup of coffee at my kitchen table only to see a child sailing down from the second story window, a dad-shirt cape wrapped around him so he could fly.

* * *

Other things were also going on in my life. I was pursuing sobriety and going to meetings. Dave should have been but it was hard to manage with the kids so he didn't. Also, he didn't talk to anyone about the things that were really going on. I guess I can understand why.

It took me a while, but I finally got a God of my understanding as suggested in the Third Step of AA. For a while there, I had od confused with my mother and I would have nothing to do with that, but over time this changed. Next, I made a dear friend, Diane, who had long, voluptuous, wavy dark hair and radiant white skin. She became my sponsor and wise mentor. A few years later, Dave introduced me to Patti when I was sober four years and she was new. Patti, tall and thin, was a teacher like the women in my family. She was the first person I met in AA that came from exactly the same world I did: Italian and fervently Catholic. Turns out my sister even went to the same church as Patti's family.

Patti, Diane and I ran together for almost ten years. We had a male friend who used to refer to us as The Triumvirate. It was great fun. The three of us ultimately separated by distance but not by heart, and they are two of my dearest friends to this day.

Somewhere along there, I finally got treated for my mental health issues. I vividly remember when I first got diagnosed with depression. My bipolar symptoms weren't evident yet, but certainly the depression was taking a continuous toll on me. I was thirty years old by then, and I had been sober for four years. Dave and I were going to marriage counseling. One week, the counselor, Pete, his name was, gave me an assignment. He told me to go home and write down ten good things about myself, and ten bad ones.

That may seem like a simple assignment, but I wasn't able to do it. I didn't even attempt to find ten bad things, although that list always seems like it would be easier. It is much easier to see the bad than the good. At the time though, I couldn't see clearly enough to even do that.

So instead of those lists, I wrote an essay. The essay was about my life and the struggles I was facing. But I remember distinctly writing about good things, or at least hopes, that someday, I would be able the overcome the fears and struggles that always seemed to face me. Something about getting the doors to life open wide once and for all.

Pete did not read the essay the day we went back. He read it before our next session, which makes sense. What surprised me was that when Dave and I went back, Pete was virtually apoplectic. He said, "The person who wrote this is very depressed! They are ready to jump off a bridge, or do something else very self-destructive, have an affair, drink or use drugs."

I was mightily surprised by this. I personally thought that what I had written was pretty optimistic. I thought, "If you think that is depressed, you should see some things I've written on other days."

Then Pete said something else interesting. "If someone I was mentoring gave this to me and I had to guess, I would never have matched this essay with you."

I had gotten so good at hiding my feelings after all my years of suffering. I wasn't trying to fool anyone, it wasn't deliberate. In my mind, I was just trying to do the best I could with what I had. I figured that's what everyone else was doing, presuming they felt like I did. Finally then, the doctor gave me medication for depression which was a huge relief. Somedays I could wake up and everything I did would not be a struggle. The new emotional freedom this gave me was dramatic.

During this period, I also surprisingly found out that I had actually graduated from college after all. At one point, I sent away for my transcripts, and the school sent back a letter saying that they couldn't send the transcripts until I paid my outstanding bill. The bill was seventeen dollars for a college diploma. I said, "What diploma???" But I sent them a check and they did indeed send me the diploma. My shame about my college career continued though. I was to remain underemployed until after the divorce.

***

As I got better, Dave got worse. He became more and more toxic. There were many incidents of phones ripped off walls or furniture smashed. If I tried to get away, he would disable the car, so we would all set off and walk to the little shop down the road until Dave would eventually calm down.

There were other incidents: a scene thrown when we went to take a professional family photograph, rocks being thrown at my car if I escaped before he disabled it. Once, after the rock incident, I left, and I would have stayed gone but I didn't see how I could manage with three kids, no money, and no place to go. I returned to that marriage and stayed for another two years.

* * *

As you can imagine, one of the strains in living in a marriage like mine is interacting with the outside world pretending life at home is normal. At home, we were always on eggshells, never knowing what might set a temper tantrum off. It was completely unpredictable, although I did my best to avoid topics that might cause trouble, money included. For years, I kept the state of our finances from Dave, paying all the bills, borrowing money from my mother. Dave was somewhat aware, he had to be, he knew what our income was, but I kept it from being in his face. I tried to keep the children away from him when he was in a bad mood, although that couldn't be avoided entirely. In some ways, it was like living with a practicing alcoholic.

In the same way as one would when living with an alcoholic, I went to great pains to make our lives appear as normal as possible on the outside. When I was very active at the children's school, none of the teachers knew what was going on at home. I was quite friendly with a number of the teachers. One of them, my son's third grade teacher, thought so highly of me that she asked me to provide daycare for her children. I thought, "If she only knew."

My close friends had some idea what was going on, but even they couldn't understand the scope of the daily tension. I always tried to put the best face on things, fed by my hope that someday, things would be different.

Sometimes the toxicity would bleed out into the outside world and there was no hiding it. Going to a restaurant was impossible. Dave was so afraid of his kids embarrassing him that he would yell at them the whole time we were there, and we were all miserable. The irony is that people would end up staring at us, probably judging us, not because of the way the children acted, but because of the way Dave himself was acting. At least, I would think, these people are strangers and I will never see them again, and I will not have to keep facing their judgment.

So I kept up appearances with my family, I kept up appearances at the kids' school, I kept up appearances with Dave's friends, just as he was doing, until it all came crashing down around us.

As with my drinking, again I was living a double life, and paying a consequent price.

* * *

Why stay in a toxic situation like the one I was in in my marriage? I have often asked myself this question, although it is somewhat of a fruitless waste of time since no one can change the past. Still, it's a question worth asking if only to learn from it. For a number of years, the biggest reason I stayed was because I thought Dave would change. Not an uncommon feeling. In truth, I loved Dave the best I was capable of at the time, and despite the troubles, I knew he loved me as best he could.

One incident in particular sticks out. Dave was raging, as he often did, although many times his toxicity was not quite so loud. I don't remember what he was raging about, but I do know it was all one-sided. I wasn't angry at him.

Dave was so far gone on this particular day that he had ripped the railing going down the stairs off the wall entirely. He was screaming about what a terrible person I was. It was as if he had morphed into the Incredible Hulk, the difference was so pronounced when he was over the edge.

All I could think was, "I know this man loves me." That was undoubtedly true. Many years later after the divorce, one of his girlfriends told me, "He never got over you." So that was my thought, I know what Dave is raging about isn't real. I reached out to him, touched him on the arm, and got his attention. I looked him steadily in the eye, and said, "Calm down. You know you don't really feel that way." I kept his eyes locked on mine, and I could literally see a film lift from over his eyes as he turned back to rationality and agreed, he didn't really feel that way. He calmed down, and we went on.

We were in counseling seven of the nine years we were married. Along the way, there were better periods and worse periods, but I kept the faith. Maybe I was naïve, but I always felt that if we stayed sober, and went to counseling, and did the work we needed to do, everything would work out okay. After all, Dave did have some good qualities and he loved his kids. Besides, with all the yelling and screaming that took place in my house growing up, I guess it didn't seem all that strange to me.

Eventually, unsurprisingly, the block we hit was Dave's childhood. In counseling, this became clear. In the final stage of our marriage, when there was a clear fork in the road, either do this and stay together, or don't do this and move apart, for whatever reason, Dave was incapable of taking the lid off the Pandora's box where his childhood lived.

Sadly, I think the biggest thing that terrified Dave was his sense that if he did open the box, he would be betraying his family. He would have to come to grips with his parents' failings, and maybe he would hate them. No child wants to betray his parents, even if the parents were abusive. This sense of loyalty may be even greater in an abused child because an abused child needs even more desperately to feel parental love.

Dave could not emotionally see past this. He didn't understand that one can acknowledge the feelings and the hurt that was inflicted and get past it to forgiveness. I believe it seemed to him that the Pandora's box would open, the feelings would come out and completely overwhelm him, and he would never get those feelings back in the box again.

Hence, for most of the nine years that we were married, I never grasped that the situation was hopeless, that there was this obstacle that could never be overcome, and so I stayed. I stayed until the truth of this could no longer be denied.

Finally, the day came when Dave gave up entirely on counseling. He just didn't want to do the things he needed to do to get better, and I can sympathize with him. Ripping off the Band-Aid straining to hold in the damage of his childhood would be devastating.

But I continued to go to counseling myself. The therapist said, "Some people come to marriage counseling to find out they need to get a divorce." I guess that was me. She also said, "You are a survivor. If you were not a survivor, you'd be dead by now." So it turns out my desire for survival had saved me, even when sometimes it was maladaptive, even though sometimes it also cost me, too.

That's what it finally came down to for me. Shortly thereafter, I was home sweeping the floor one day and somehow it came to me. It was too toxic for me in that house. I knew deep down inside then that I would have to drink to survive it.

That's when I knew that marriage was over.

* * *

As I was working through all these feelings, I had removed myself from the bedroom. I slept on the couch in the living room for three months. Other than that, things seemed to go on like normal, at least the kids never questioned it. But as if I didn't have enough troubles, another incident occurred during this time that was to alter a whole family.

For most of the time we were married, Dave's father Sam and I had had a good relationship. Sam was old and weathered from all his years as a bricklayer working out in the sun. He always greeted my children with a jesting, "Hey, turkey!" That's the one thing they still remember about him, they were young when he died.

Sam was very supportive of me. He was well aware that Dave and I were having serious troubles. One day, troubled as things were, Sam offered to take me and the kids out to a restaurant for lunch.

When we went to lunch, Sam's behavior was passing strange, and it got worse as the day went on. While we were in the car, Sam kept putting his hand on my leg. It made me extremely uncomfortable. Then we had to stop at Sam's apartment for some reason, and while we were there, when the kids were in another room, Sam grabbed me and started kissing me.

When this happened, the bottom fell out from under me. I couldn't believe what was happening. I felt like I went into another state of shock like I had so many years ago on that fateful day with my brother. It was an unwanted advance, for one thing. Furthermore, it was an unwanted advance from a parental figure, one who was both a parental figure to me, and a parental figure who was deeply betraying his own son. And it was happening with my children in the room right next door.

I managed to extricate myself from that situation as best as I could, but then as I always did, I just went on. Sam and I and the kids all went to lunch, the world screeching dizzily around me.

Knowing how badly this would hurt Dave, I didn't tell him right away. I did tell my girlfriends, I had to, it's as if I had been violated again. But I was never a person who could manage dishonesty very well. Eventually I felt like I couldn't live with the secret anymore, and I did tell Dave. Poor Dave! He had so much on his plate already, and was already in such a hurt place due to the state of our relationship. I just couldn't do anything different, I know only too well that secrets can be fatal.

Soon after, Dave confronted his father who denied it. Dave and I had big arguments about this. Dave wanted me to take the accusation back, but I couldn't. Maybe there was some other explanation for Sam's behavior, I said. Sam suffered from terrible diabetes. Maybe Sam's blood sugar was out of whack that day. Maybe it was something else. Maybe he didn't know what he was doing, maybe he doesn't remember it. That was all I could give. But even on the verge of the divorce, and even in the midst of dealing with my own feelings over what had happened, to me the situation between Dave and his father was heartrending.

Later that year, amid much sadness and denial, Sam gradually deteriorated physically. That same year, Sam passed away.

Dave and his family blamed me for this, and probably some of them still do. I don't hold this against them, I can understand why they would feel that way. Somehow to this day, I only see cosmically tragic victims in this, all of us, even Sam. He was just a victim of a terrible loneliness, a loneliness which had, for a moment, blinded his judgment.

Of all my many stories, to me this is one of the saddest. The anguish it brought forever altered a whole other desperate, wildly dysfunctional family, not just me.

* * *

The end of a marriage is always traumatic, even under the best of circumstances. I've always wondered why some people think divorce is this easy way out. Even disregarding the obvious financial and other consequences, the decision is difficult emotionally. The sense of loss for me when I decided to get a divorce was crushing. The end meant the loss of dreams, the final acknowledgment of the loss of the man I married, the man who had been funny and fun and smart and a good dancer, a man I knew loved me. It all seemed so unnecessary to me, but there it was. All the things I had planned and hoped for, raising children together, standing together at their graduations and their weddings, sharing holidays with the family, standing shoulder to shoulder in the face of life's ups and downs, all gone, broken into a million different pieces left in shards all around me.

Even when a divorce is unavoidable, even when there is no other alternative and the choice is clear, the sense of loss is profound. When I decided to divorce, I felt a literal breaking of my heart. It felt like a wine-press was pressing down on my chest, the weight a solid core between my rib cage, squeezing around my back like a rubber band and radiating up my chest over my lungs. I would rock in pain for hours in a rocking chair thinking, "What happened to the man I married?"

Despite how some people see it, divorce is rarely easy. Maybe it is for some people, but that's not the way it was for me. Even today, the losses associated with my first divorce still cut deeply.

* * *

When I finally informed Dave of my decision to divorce, he was surprised. In his hurt, he would say, "I had no idea this was coming." I know he truly felt that way. Somehow his own denial mechanism had blanked out the fact that I hadn't shared a bedroom with him in months. Our brains will do strange things to us sometimes, only allowing us to see the things we are capable of handling emotionally and nothing else.

Obviously, Dave had a different opinion about the divorce. He did not want the marriage to be over. There were veiled threats about 'til death do us part.' I was very grateful he didn't like guns. So how could I get him to leave? I had already tried leaving myself and knew there wasn't any way I could manage leaving with all three kids. Dave didn't want to leave. So what could I do?

Finally, I devised a plan. I told Dave that if he didn't leave, I would leave, and I would leave the kids with him. That terrified him. While he loved his kids, he never took care of them. So he agreed to go.

I remember the day clearly. At age thirty-five, I sat at my neighbor's kitchen window and watched Dave as he moved his stuff out. I don't really know how the kids felt about it. I think they understood. I think maybe they were relieved, although no child wants to see their parents divorced. I myself was terribly sad that day. But I also thought that life would be better this way, and I would be safe.

I was wrong.

* * *

And that was the end of The Happy Family, and the beginning of The Disaster.

The boys when they were little. From left to right, Dominic with his button eyes, Little Dave with his Ninja turtles, and Patrick at a birthday party.

The last picture we took as a family, 1994.

CHAPTER 11

The Disaster

One of the hardest things about the divorce was that we were poor. Funny how I never thought of us that way. In the back of my mind, I always thought of us as 'temporarily cash-strapped.' Ingrained in me was the idea of my own childhood, where, as miserly as my mother was, we did know financial security. But what the kids remember is that we were poor. I never really realized that until lately when two of them said something about it on two different occasions. It kind of hurt when they said that, I'm not sure why.

But poor we were. I was still working at a doctor's office, the pay was small, and then I moved on to teaching at a Catholic school, where the pay was also small. By this time, Big Dave was making plenty of money as my mother had paid for him to go to computer school, and he, as smart as he was, was good at it. But he was not going to share that largess with us, no matter that my mother was responsible for it. He had his fear of financial insecurity going on, plus there was no way he was ever going to do anything to help me. In his mind, I was out to get him for his money. Somehow it never occurred to him that this would hurt his children, too.

Hence, in the divorce settlement, I agreed to take less than half of what he should have been paying for child support, mostly because by that point, I was in fear for my life. Being poor was better than being dead. My sister had gotten a law degree by then (just one of her many degrees), and she worked on the divorce, and went along with letting Dave misrepresent his income. So instead of paying child support, Dave bought thirty thousand dollars worth of guitars when the kids were wearing rags, and he and others blamed me for the rags, including his mother. At the time, I never saw the injustice in this. In my mind, I went along with it, too. The feeling that I was always to blame for everything was deeply ingrained in me. My mother had told me so since I was small child. In this case, my mother blamed me for the Big D, the Divorce, since I was the one who had asked Dave to leave.

We did get assistance. My kids qualified for Medicaid, we got Earned Income Credit, the kids got free lunch at school, I got free childcare so I could continue to work, my mother helped me some as did my Aunt Elsie. My cousin Katherine would bring us bags of food, that's when my kids started calling her Laffy Kathy. She always did bring laughter her with her. That was good because we needed laughter. There are some things in life that charity can't fix. I have a surreal image in my head of going to Toys for Tots to pick out Christmas presents. All I can tell you is that is not the same as a real Christmas, and actually, it felt quite tragic.

Yesterday, one son told me that one of the things he most blames my sister for is that she never helped us. Her family had plenty, yet Betsy never did one thing to help us financially. At the time, it didn't seem odd to me, I guess I didn't expect it of her because then where would it end for her? But Katherine and Aunt Elsie helped us, so obviously it was possible. Maybe Betsy could have showered the kids with lots of presents at Christmas. But she did nothing, and continued to do mostly nothing throughout my life whenever I was in trouble. So much for being a 'Saint Sister,' which, funnily enough, I always thought she was. I was always telling people how nice Katherine and Betsy were, as they were born a day apart, and it was in both their astrological signs to be kind. I was always telling my kids, "My sister is a very nice person." Now I understand why they never believed me, although this was only one of the reasons. The other was her predilection for being judgmental which would later become quite obvious.

So much for the thin veneer of being 'perfect'.

* * *

All I can say is that for my kids, being poor changed them, as did the divorce. Being poor and coming from a broken family shames you. I don't think my kids ever got over that even to this day.

Eventually, I got a good career, but by the time I did, it was too late for them. I wrote a poem about that during this time period, though nominally it was about my mother. I said I hoped that it would not be too late for them when the time came that life would get better for us, but by the time my career change came, sadly, it was.

* * *

Undoubtedly, the worst part of the divorce was the violence. Despite my very real grief after Dave left, I went out looking for a man. I still had a Man Thing after all, and I hadn't learned my lesson yet. There were various flirtations. Ultimately, I ended up with Joe.

He was the uncle of my third-tier friend Margaret from grade school. He was older and slightly taller than me, with thick graying hair that suited his profession. He was a steelworker, a devoted member of the steelworkers union. He smelled of old-timey aftershave like my father occasionally had.

At the time, Joe was still married. That didn't bother me at all although it should have. I figured if their marriage wasn't working out, and they had real problems of their own, then it wasn't my problem. I like to think I paid for this during my second divorce when all my friends betrayed me. Hopefully so. Karma is a bitch.

Joe and I didn't start dating until Dave and I had been separated for about ten months. By then I had gotten what

Maryland calls a Limited Divorce. Basically, this means you can do anything except remarry, at least that's what a lawyer told me. You can't get a Final Divorce in Maryland until you've been separated for at least a year, but I thought I was free to date. Dave disagreed with me; he called it adultery.

For a time, Dave had been pretty peaceful. In fact, he was on his best behavior. He was desperately hoping for a reconciliation, but my psyche had completely closed the door on that by then. He never understood. It was never going to work out that way. But when I started dating someone else, that's when the shit hit the fan.

In a way, I can understand why Dave lost it. Joe had been a friend of his as well, so it was a double betrayal. What followed was a lot of very real threats, and an unsuccessful suicide attempt by Dave which ended him up in a hospital. The hospital let Dave out too early. The day Dave got out, he called our house every hour and continued well into the night. Joe was at my house with me. Diane always said that Joe had a need to be a white knight. He liked being the one to save the damsel in distress which, in this case, was me. It had to be so. There is no other reason any man would put their life in danger like that. Especially not for me. Not that I didn't deserve it, but Joe and I, while we liked each other a lot, did not have anything like a soul-mate thing going on, so putting his life on the line should not have been worth it.

Dave threatened to come over that night, and the next day, come over he did. Mind you, Dave was a great big scary guy weighing in at two hundred and forty lbs. Joe, on the other hand, was not much bigger than me. Any physical contest was never going to be a fair fight, especially not fueled by Dave's insane rage.

First, Dave tried to kick down the sliding glass door at the back of the house. Joe didn't want the kids to see that, so he figured he would just go out to talk to Dave. Joe went out the front door which was surrounded by a little alcove, and Dave met him there. Dave flew into his rage. He picked Joe up like a rag doll and threw him again and again against the walls of the alcove. Inside the house, all we could do was listen to the thumping. The kids were eleven, eight, and four by then, and they were all there for it.

When all was said and done, after Dave's rage had been spent, he left Joe lying in the alcove in a bloody mess the kids had to step over to escape to the neighbor's house. Dave went away in a police car and spent three days in jail. Joe went away in an ambulance. Fortunately, he had not sustained any serious injuries, but surely, he could have.

* * *

This little incident was enough for the courts to give me a restraining order, not that those really do any good if someone is bent on destruction. Still, the pattern of harassment continued until one day, Dave said he was coming to the house again. I had been letting the children see him every other weekend. I figured they were his one tether to reality. One of the kids had left a toy at Dave's house on a visit. According to Dave, it was very important that the child, I don't remember which one, had that toy returned to him. I knew deep in my heart that this would be dangerous. My sister had been talking to Dave on the phone about the divorce settlement, and even she called to warn me. We called the police. The police were there when Dave came. Thankfully, that sobered Dave enough to go home because I dread to think what else could have happened that day to all of us.

In general, though, Dave was undeterred. He would follow me in his car when I would drive to the store. We did the only thing we could do We went into hiding, Joe and I, and the three kids. But we had to come back sometime, right?

So we waited until the courts were open. They had been closed for a week due to a snowstorm. We got a quick court date for violation of the restraining order. When the court date came, Dave and I both showed up. First, I told of my experiences. I related the stories of the time Dave had come to the house, and when he had followed me. The judge was actually on Dave's side at first. He said there was no issue when the police came because nothing happened. Then the judge said Dave might coincidentally have been going to the same shopping center as I was for something else when it appeared he was following me.

Then Dave got on the stand. He was so far gone that he ranted and raved about how I had been provoking him when he followed me. He blamed it all on me. Finally, the judge thankfully saw the truth of it and told Dave that he better get his shit together or he would go to jail for two months. Dave had been to jail already, he didn't want that, so things got a little bit better.

***

Still things were bad. Things were so chaotic that I considered putting the kids in foster care temporarily, but I couldn't figure out how to do it so I could be sure I could get them back. Dear Patti left runaway money in my car in case I needed to run again. Although I had stopped going to church by then, I went and had Masses said for Dave. Bad as it sounds, I prayed, "Please let Dave get better, or please let him die," because we couldn't go on living like this. I did continue to let Dave see the kids, for the same reason as before, but we had to exchange them at the police station.

When that restraining order expired, Dave started to act up again, but I took him back to court, representing myself, and though I didn't get another order, the threat was enough to get Dave at least a little straightened out. Dave just went back to making my life as difficult as he possibly could in any other way, not helping me with money, not helping me in any way with the kids if I needed it, or in any other way he could think of.

Sadly for Dave, he wasn't out of touch with this reality later on in his life and his older years were unhappy. By the time Dave was fifty, he was retired on disability. His body was falling apart, his spine destroyed by his years playing football. He also had severe diabetes and heart disease. He was in a lot of pain all the time, had wounds on his feet that wouldn't heal, and had surgery after surgery for various things. Often, the hospital in FL would call up to my house to get permission to treat Dave from my eighteen-year-old son, Pat, who couldn't understand what was happening and didn't know what to say. Dave's muscular build was only a memory.

Dave knew by then that what he had done when the children were young was wrong. One of his friends once said, "She tried to have you put in jail." And he said, "No, I did." He later went on with Little Dave about how he knew he had deliberately set out to be destructive to me, not realizing that the harder he made my life, the harder he was making life for his kids. Little Dave told me about this, although now Little Dave doesn't remember. And to whatever small degree possible for Big Dave, he did love his kids.

The physical and emotional pain Dave was in by the time he was in his fifties proved to be too much for him. Big Dave committed suicide when he was fifty eight.

* * *

My family had different reactions to the divorce. Of course, my mother blamed me. In fact, one Thanksgiving when we went to her house to visit, all she could talk about was how she missed Dave. He even called my mother's house, and she was in the background yelling, "Tell him that we miss him!" At the time, I was in real fear of him killing me. I once told her later, "Mom, that's the only thing in life I feel you owe me an apology for. Taking Dave's side when he was trying to murder me."

My sister and I weren't close, but I still viewed Betsy as the benevolent, if emotionally distant, aunt. She did help with the legal stuff for the divorce, and on the one day Dave was so dangerous, she did call to warn me. Later sometimes, Betsy would babysit for my kids. Recently, my sons and I found out that Betsy told her own sons she had to do this because my family was poor. My sons had thought it was because their cousins loved them.

Tony came to visit. The old stuff between us had fallen away by then even though I was still suffering the consequences. Tony intimated that if I needed someone to take Dave out, he knew people who could do that for me. I suppose that was his way of protecting me.

Chris was nowhere to be found. He had married by then

and had a daughter. I only saw Chris or talked to him at family celebrations or on holidays. On those occasions, a patronizing pretense at affection had replaced his frank disapproval of me. We only ever talked about trivial things. Under normal circumstances, that was true for all of us. By the time of my divorce, Chris was no doubt somewhere feeling very superior to me, although by then, he had his own marital problems.

* * *

I believe we all have a spiritual longing in us, a desire for our own connection to God-ness. For me, that had started with the Echo program in high school, maybe even when I ran away to the sanctuary when I was twelve. I believe if we allow ourselves to remain open to it, the call in us will be fulfilled. Sometimes not in the way we expect it, and not all the time.

Why we do not have it all the time is Mystery. I would just as soon it not be that way. There's the old Footprints story, the story where there are two sets of footprints in the sand, but when the gentleman has some trouble, he sees only one set of footprints. He asks God why He had abandoned him. God replies, "That is when I was carrying you."

Personally, those are the times I wish God were even more visible, not invisible, but certainly I have had times of a crisis of faith where God is not visible at all. The fact that sometimes we feel connected to God and sometimes not, even when we are sincerely praying, may be a Mystery we will never understand. Sometimes in life, we must find a way to accept that Mystery, the unknowingness of the unknowable.

I myself have had three serious crises of faith in sobriety where God seemed nowhere to be found. One was during my worst depression, one came after I walked down a specific path I thought was being put before me by God but turned out badly, and one had to do with my kids when they grew up. These are never periods I enjoy. Somewhat surprisingly, I did not have one about Dave.

In fact, right after Dave left, I took to rocking Pat during his nap. The whole nap, up to three hours. I would rock him and stare out the window at the sky. Patti could never understand how I could do that. While I was doing that, a Being I call The African Mother God came to me. She was an old, wrinkled African shaman type. In my mind, I would envision that She would lay me down on a mat by a river and chant spells over me for healing and anoint me with healing oils. She stayed with me in my life for quite some time. It became a saying or joke with my friends. If something good happened, we would say, "The African Mother God is doing that!"

I had a God experience.

* * *

After the divorce, I also had my dear friends close to me. After Dave left but before things got crazy, Diane lived with me. (That was when she started calling me Queenie. Me, bossy much?) Tina was right next door with her kids. Patti was a five-minute drive away. I had what Diane likes to refer to as 'a nest,' and it was very good for me. I had medication for depression and the bipolar part hadn't become prominent yet. So life went on, as it always did in my life, even after terrible things had happened to me. Joe went back to his wife, and that was best for everybody.

* * *

And that was the end of The Disaster. Serious mental illness was yet to come.

A recent picture of Joe, who risked his life for me.

CHAPTER 12

Jesus, and Mental Illness

By the time the dust from my divorce had settled, I realized that it was about time I did something about my work situation. I had worked in low-paying jobs in doctors' offices for ten years which is bad when you are a single mother. I do give some credit to the first of those jobs in supporting me when I first stopped drinking. They loved me, and as usual for me in that type of environment, I had bloomed.

But the time had come to move on. I decided to go into teaching as it was a family thing. It was what my mother had done although she had become a clinical psychologist by then, go figure. I always thought my mother subconsciously did that so she could figure out what went wrong with her children. My sister had dabbled with the law but had gone back to teaching, and my aunt had been a teacher for fifty years before her death. So teaching seemed right for me. I wasn't going to go back to undergraduate school to become qualified, I already had a degree (surprise!), so I decided to go to grad school to get a Master's in Teaching at a nearby college.

I was a little concerned about this career change, and was carrying a lot of baggage from my divorce. When I got my first teaching job at a Catholic school where I could work as I finished my degree, I was very nervous. We happened to have our twentieth high school reunion that year, and there I ran into Sr. Pieta, one of my old high school teachers. I relayed all my troubles to her, and all the things I felt guilty about, and she said in a very emphatic way, "Regina, you just have to get over that." Easier said than done.

Teaching didn't work out for me. That's its own long story, but suffice to say that after that school year ended, a job fell into my lap. It was a job as a technical writer, exactly what my degree was in, engineering science with a minor in journalism. It came open right at the very time I needed it, and my neighbor told me about it. It was at her employer's. I always attribute this coincidence to 'God serendipity.' The job was slightly higher paying. The Catholic school had not paid much better than the doctors' offices, so this was a real gift to me. I worked at that technical writing job until I moved to another area and was employed elsewhere. Finally, I had a career.

* * *

By this time, God also saw fit to send me on another journey. It was very strange how it happened, because if I had known certain things, it is a path I would never have chosen to walk. It started with Patti. She was married, but she also like to 'look.' It was always a big joke for us. She had met a man, David (yes, another David!) at a meeting who she thought was so good-looking that he was to die for. Patti talked about David a lot but mentioned he had some legal troubles and might have to go to jail. Not unusual for someone in AA.

I never thought much more about David, but one of the times I happened to be in court for the divorce, there he was. The guards brought him in in chains and shackles. He was so ashamed he wouldn't even look at me. I felt so bad for him. I knew what that kind of shame feels like. Then I had to leave the courtroom for a minute, so I never found out what he 'was in for.'

Also coincidentally, I knew a man, Willy, who was very instrumental in my own sobriety, the man who had welcomed me back when I first felt I was home in AA. Turns out Willy was very close to David. He encouraged me to write David, otherwise I never would have, I would never have known how to contact him. Willy didn't tell me what David's crime was either.

So I started writing David. A jailhouse romance seemed like the perfect thing for me. No, not ideal circumstances, but since I had felt a strong connection to David in the courtroom, it was enough. Enough to satisfy my Man-Thing. Enough to make me feel lovable.

Writing David soon progressed to jailhouse visits. I cherished him. He was sweet, kind, self-effacing. He had a sheepish, shy, crooked smile, and straight brown hair parted in the middle, winging off to the sides. He was tall like the men in my family.

David and I got to know each other better, and I was still wondering what he was in for. He was very reluctant to share with me, but I shared some of my deepest secrets with him. Eventually he told me he was in for molesting his stepson.

If I had heard this before I fell in love with David, I would never have gotten involved with him. That's why I say this was a God thing. God got me out of that courtroom so I didn't hear that day, and God hooked me up with Willy to get in contact with him.

By the time I heard Dave's story, I had already fallen in love, and it was true love. I loved David deeply. I even shared with him what happened with my brother, which very, very few people knew about back then. Even right down to the gory details. This was somewhat cathartic for me, although I had already dealt with some of it. Then we decided David needed the same kind of catharsis because he still felt a great deal of shame about what he had done. So David wrote a twenty-page missive to me. Actually, he told me about what had happened to him when he was a child, because as is common, he had been a victim before he was an abuser.

Nothing could have prepared me for what I got. Without going into details, I will just say that it was far more terrible than what had happened to me. And it had happened with men.

Then I knew. Whatever David had done had to have been

more terrible than anything that I had imagined, which was relatively benign, if you can ever say that about such a thing. This completely freaked me out. I hadn't been diagnosed as bipolar yet, but I'm sure I had a mixed manic episode. A mixed episode means a person has the energy of a manic episode but without the euphoria. The feelings are all negative instead. In this state, I literally did not sleep for a week. I was living in agony, replaying the unforgiveable possibilities over and over and over again in my head. Eventually, I did hear the whole story, and it was every bit as unforgiveable as I feared it would be. I was still teaching at this time, and I can say for a fact that it is very difficult to teach under those circumstances, but teach I did.

What came to me then was The Dream, and I think this is what God was trying to teach me. I had always been very judgmental about these things, although weirdly I forgave my brother. I always thought that child abusers must certainly be among those who go to hell. I was, in fact, adamant about that when I talked to Diane about it, not knowing someone else who had been an abuser was listening when I said that. Effectively I would have doomed David, the other guy and everyone else like that to go to hell, including my brother, too, for that matter.

As an aside, most people who do things like that have been a victim themselves, even my brother as I had found out. Hurt people hurt. As David's lawyer later told me, in cases like David, we are not talking about a sexual predator but rather about a person making a cry for help. That was the part I didn't understand. Therefore, I judged, at least until The Dream.

In my dream, the setting was the scene in the Bible with Jesus and Barabbas, the one where Pontius Pilate is going to release a Jew as a token gift in honor of an upcoming Jewish holiday. In the Bible version, Pontius Pilate sends both Jesus and Barabbas out to the Jewish crowd to let the crowd decide which one of them would live, and which one of them would die. "Which one do you want to live," Pontius Pilate said, "Jesus or Barabbas?" The crowd shouts 'Barabbas!' And again and again the question is asked and again and again, the crowd shouts, "Barabbas!" So

Jesus was the one chosen to die.

My dream was a little bit different. In my dream, Pontius Pilate was there, and so was Jesus. But instead of Barabbas, the other man was David. In this dream, Pontius Pilate was asking the crowd, "Which one do you want to die? Jesus or the Child Defiler? Jesus or the Child Defiler?" Again and again.

My reference to anyone like David was never 'child defiler,' and it in no way reflected any way I ever thought about this. This is one of the things that convinces me that this dream came straight from God.

In my dream, I was somehow present for this scene, a watching bystander, although it wasn't really like I was there. I was watching like it was theatre, I would say. In this dream, when asked which one should die, Jesus or the Child Defiler, the crowd kept saying, "Jesus! Jesus! Jesus!" And I thought in my head, Jesus isn't going to be very happy about that. Somehow Jesus heard me. He looked directly at me at said, "No, this is what I came here for. This is what I am for." Further, He looked at David and said, 'This day you shall be with me in Heaven.' Metaphorically speaking in Dave's case, I guess. So David was forgiven, and Jesus looked at me, too, and then I knew I was forgiven, for the sins I had committed and even the ones I was the victim of. My soul was infused with peace.

This was my second tangible God experience, and I feel very fortunate to have had it.

***

Up until this dream, I had never understood why Jesus had to die on a cross. It didn't make any sense to me. He could just say we were forgiven and be done with it. But then I felt that the combined sins of men, before Him and after Him, were so great that only a river could wash them away, and it was a river of blood, Jesus's blood.

I haven't been in a church in a very long time, and even then, only for ceremonies like weddings or funerals. I may never be in a church again. Also, I have had other forms of God appear to me, so I don't really think you can call me strictly Christian.

But I can say this: I know Jesus, and I know what Jesus is about, and that is Love and Forgiveness. And it's all because God sent me on the journey, by coincidence and serendipity, so obviously, it was a lesson I needed to learn. We should all learn it.

Thus, finally coming to this understanding, I forgave David. His crime was not against me, nonetheless I had to find forgiveness in my heart to make peace with it. David's family, including his stepson, was able to forgive David, too.

***

My relationship with David continued after this. I still loved David, and David was learning to love himself. I went on to see him in jail for another several years although going to the jail was an ordeal in and of itself. The jail was an hour and a half away, and the process for getting checked in for a visit was arduous. After check-in, there was a long walk to the visiting room. I would necessarily trudge through multiple drab beige hallways and locked metal doors, the doors sliding and buzzing and clanging as they opened and closed to let us through. While walking, I always felt a mixture of anticipation coupled with the discomfort of knowing this was not normal, that normal people did not live like this. Normal people were not constantly being scrutinized on their way to see a criminal who was incarcerated. In a way, jail visits were a place out of time that carried an underlying sadness that was inescapable.

Once inside the visiting room, I would wait for David to arrive after he went through the regular indignity of being strip searched before the visit. The room was open and had long narrow counters, each with a small, six-inch wood barrier. We weren't allowed to touch during the visit, we only got a hug and a kiss at beginning of the visit and at the end. On holidays, we could pay to get pictures and the guards let us stand together and hold hands. At Christmas, the jail even provided a meal, and we could actually sit and have dinner together. The enjoyment was tempered as we knew it would soon be over and we would be back counting the seemingly endless days before David would be free.

The lack of true physical connection during the visits was always underneath, always hiding between our conversations, always taunting us, always leaving us lonely even though we were both there.

Few and as lonely as they we, every visit was precious. David and I could only visit once a week. In-between there were only short, expensive prison phone calls and intimate letters that by their very nature when they were written could only be one half of the conversation.

But we made the best of things. During our precious visits, David and I talked about everything, we talked about God, we talked about us and the fairytale future we were going to have when he got out (evidently, I still believed in fairytales after all), we had visits with Willy, and with David's mother and his daughter. We discussed the possibility David was gay given his life experience. He said he didn't think he was. I told him, "If you are gay, and you don't own it, you will never be whole." Diane later said that's not really a question you can answer when you are in jail given the adverse circumstances. So for a while, our fairytale played on.

By this time, you can probably guess where this is going, but I certainly didn't. Finally, finally David got out, what a happy day! We had one romantic weekend, and then the inevitable happened, although I didn't know it was that.

David disappeared, and I didn't know why.

It took about three weeks for David to fully disappear, and when he did, I completely lost it. I tried and tried to call him at his mother's house where he was staying but she would never put me through to him. I wrote letter after letter with no response.

I know the reaction of many people was that they were not surprised. It's probably pretty common for a jailbird to use someone trusting like me while they are in jail, taking what they need while they are incarcerated with no intention of anything afterwards. While some people thought that, this explanation just didn't fit for me. David and I had shared too deeply about our lives. It just didn't make sense to me. I wracked and wracked my brains trying to understand it but somehow, I could not. A poem I wrote at the time explains it better:

Any minute now,
Someone is going to come and wake me up
And tell me it's all been a bad dream.
"Shew," I'll say,
"What a relief.
I was having such a hard time making sense of it."
It's as if, in an instant,
I was warped to an alternate reality
Where "1 + 1 = 3."
Now the walls and floors and ceilings
Don't fit together right
And I am trapped
In this horrific carnival funhouse scenery.
I can't walk straight.
I can't see my way.
I keep crashing into the funhouse mirror,
The merry-go-round music is screeching,
The world is laughing hysterically
And the shattering joke
Is on me.

That's the way I felt, as if reality had totally warped around me. It didn't help that my dearest friend, Diane, the one I always relied on to explain things to me, had moved to North Carolina almost exactly at that time. It sounds odd in the time of cellphones, but they weren't common at that time, so Diane wasn't even available by phone for quite some time.

One way I handled this was to write. I wrote voluminous pages to myself, my moods fluctuating rapidly between rage and bewilderment. On the one hand, I was enraged by the thought of David abandoning me. On the surface, it seemed he had taken advantage of me, and there was an intense sense of betrayal. The rage burned hot but at least when I was enraged, it kept the pain away. On the other hand, I was bewildered and despairing because I just didn't understand how David could have abandoned me after all that we had shared together. This circumstance brought back the deep feelings of the rejection I had had from Tony. David's rejection unfolded inside me bearing a weight that would pull me under. The two feelings, anger and despair, went rapid cycling, back and forth, back and forth, jolting and pulling, careening off the rails. On top of everything else, not knowing my future diagnosis, I was completely at a loss to explain what was happening, even to myself.

Even at work, I would write, the feelings pouring out in a flood before me. It was beyond my power to stop it. That's when everything in my brain starting rhyming, and the rhyming went on for weeks. My brain was always racing but underneath it, I was getting physically exhausted. I felt a jittery tension coupled with an underlying weariness as if I had been drinking espresso all day and then wasn't able to sleep at night, only with no end in sight. I could feel the exhaustion intensely, but I couldn't do anything about it. When you are manic or mixed manic as I was, you cannot sleep. Ultimately, my state of mental, physical and emotional exhaustion became extreme.

I guess in a normal person, over time the feelings would become less pronounced even if still difficult. The situation would stabilize some. That's not what happened for me. My mood changes just kept escalating, rapidly switching between a horrible anger and a horrible despair.

Some alcoholics at this point might have seen a return to drinking as a solution to this, but I never considered it. I knew in my heart of hearts that drinking would only make things worse.

It may seem odd to some people, but I never discussed the situation with my family. This is perfectly understandable in my case. My family was one to simply tell me to buck up and sweep things like this under the rug. My family would have been completely incapable of understanding or supporting me.

I also hadn't seen a psychologist or psychiatrist in quite

some time. I was still getting medication for depression, but my primary care physician was prescribing it. I saw him infrequently, he didn't know me very well, and I didn't feel like he would understand what I was going through, so I did not contact him.

Eventually, though, it got to the point where something drastic needed to be done. I won't say I was suicidal really, but I got to the point where I couldn't function. There I was, exhausted and jittery, writing and rhyming, my kids and my job completely fading from my sense of perception.

With no escape and no one to talk to, I decided to go to a hospital. It seemed drastic, but it also seemed like the only available option, and my only hope.

Afterwards, when I did discuss it with my family, I remarked to my sister that some people probably would think that picking up a six pack of beer was the easier, less drastic and more logical solution, but I knew it wasn't for me, and with this, she absolutely agreed.

* * *

Walking into an emergency room all alone when in a distraught state is an experience you never forget. My heart was pounding, my hands were shaking, and my vision was blurry as I walked in through the shiny sliding glass doors. The triage nurse looked at me funny, all alone there in my condition, but my external perception had faded and I was beyond the point where I could care.

Eventually, the ER staff took me back to the room to see the doctor. I didn't understand at all what was happening to me, and I guess I couldn't explain it very well. The first thing the doctor and social worker told me was that they couldn't admit me because the criteria for hospital admission is being a threat to yourself or someone else. I had told them I wasn't suicidal. Hence, I didn't qualify.

With that, the last hope I had been clinging to disappeared, fluttering impotently away before my very eyes. Hopeless. What occurred to me then was if I couldn't be in the hospital, I would just go lie down in the street in front of the hospital and let a car run over me.

On hearing that, the doctors changed their minds. They would admit me to the hospital after all.

As it turned out, the hospital was a disgusting place. I couldn't even use the phone as it had what I can only call slime all over it. The doctor wasn't familiar to me and I don't think even the professionals really understood what I was going through. Looking back, what I needed for a couple of days was sedation, and they didn't do that for me. They just woke me up in the morning to go to groups that I couldn't even connect to. Still, I did stabilize somewhat having a few days when I had no other responsibilities I had to take care of.

While my treatment was lacking, something did happen to me at that hospital. I would never have considered myself bipolar, but while I was there, I heard a nurse say to another man when she was giving him his medication, "This is for your mood swings." I couldn't think it terms of bipolar but mood swings I could relate to, so while I was in the hospital, the doctor decided to give me something for mood swings, too.

* * *

While the immediate crisis was over, I still cried about David. I cried about him a lot. I would go on long walks through the neighborhood, sobbing and sobbing. Lord knows what the neighbors thought of me. But as I walked and cried, something came to me. Something, some sort of intuition, told me there was more going on with David than what I could see. I had that God-sense that I was about to find out.

Sure enough, somehow by coincidence, I found out where David was working and I called him there instead of his mother's house. David took my call! We made arrangements for me to go to David's workplace to see him. I was overjoyed. I loved him after all.

When David and I met, the secret came out. The mystery was finally solved. David told me that when he got out, he realized he was gay, and he had been afraid to tell me. Then David thanked me profusely. He said, "Regina, remember when you said that to me about being whole? That's what did it for me. When I got out and these feelings came over me, I just knew I had to find out because I wanted to be whole." But I'll give God the credit for that, too.

David and I went our separate ways, it was too hard to manage my romantic feelings for him any other way. I just couldn't make the switch to seeing him platonically, and he had joined a social world of men I could not easily be a part of. Continuing to see him always felt like a reminder of an unbearable loss to me.

But for a little while, David and I kept in touch, and on Valentine's Day, he would call and tell me that he loved me.

* * *

Another somewhat-miracle happened during this time. While all this was going on and I was going to hospitals and crying and crying and crying, my mother (my mother, not someone else and their mother, my mother) softly said to me,

"My beautiful daughter, no one should ever hurt my beautiful daughter."

I was forty-one.

* * *

And that was the story of Jesus, and Mental Illness. But then, there was worse mental illness to come.

*David and I on Valentine's Day at the jail.
A rare moment when we could stand side by side.*

CHAPTER 13

More Mental Illness and Men

So I was bipolar. When I first heard that diagnosis, I had trouble believing it. How do you know you're bipolar? It's not an illness that causes you any pain, or that you recognize as causing you pain. I just thought I was having 'mood swings.'

When the doctor officially first said I was bipolar, I went home and googled everything about bipolar, trying to see if it fit me, if it fit my experience. Some of the things I found I could relate to, but some of it I couldn't. I did find something about rhyming though, and that convinced me. I also found a book called *An Unquiet Mind* by Kay Redfield Jamison. It's an excellent book written by a woman who is bipolar herself. If you want to know more about bipolar illness, I highly recommend it.

I didn't have everything in common with the author, such as her manic shopping or her supportive family, but she did relate instances of having Post-It-Notes everywhere in a manic episode, and that helped convinced me also because I had done that, too.

My mother didn't believe my diagnosis either, although by then, she was a licensed clinical psychologist. It's not that she wasn't capable of understanding my diagnosis. It just didn't fit her narrative about the perfect family. She saw it as some reflection on her, true narcissist that she was.

I actually was aware of this perspective of hers. I'd had a lot of experience with it and a lot of therapy. I tap-danced around it. I told my mother that while I was bipolar, obviously my illness didn't come from her side of the family. It had to have come from Dad's. After all, I had a grandfather who committed suicide, right? She said, "He wasn't depressed, he just had a bad life." Denial ain't a river in Egypt. Thank goodness she was only my mother and not my doctor.

* * *

Looking back now, my bipolar symptoms seem obvious, and it seems odd that I did not get diagnosed sooner. I had been seeing a psychiatrist off and on for ten years by the time I got diagnosed as bipolar, which was somewhere around the time I turned forty, give or take a bit. However, there were some symptoms I didn't readily recognize, primarily hypo-mania, so I never talked to a doctor about them. Hypo-mania is a mild form of a manic episode, but I didn't recognize it. I just knew I felt really good sometimes and got a lot accomplished. My judgment was not impaired. Over time though, I think my moods swings must have gotten more serious.

The year just prior to my diagnosis is illustrative of my progression. There were several warning signs that year. One, I had a work project to do where I wildly exceeded expectations. This was the era of the Post-It-Note. I was writing about processes for funding disbursement for the Navy. Yes, a rather dry subject, but I was consumed by it. There were many complications for that process, not surprising considering the level of bureaucracy and red tape in the government. I was piecing it all together and I would think of things while I was driving home that I didn't want to forget so while I was driving fifty miles an hour, I was writing Post-It-Notes and sticking them on the steering wheel. Obviously, this was dangerous. Eventually I got a tape recorder.

The written end result of this overall work effort received resounding applause. I even got to go to the beach that year to stay in the company condo in North Carolina. That's a bonus the company used to give out for exceptional service. This was as the result of a manic episode.

A few months after that episode, I flipped and had the reverse. There came a depression triggered by the death of John F. Kennedy, Jr. I was inconsolable. It was as if a dear friend or close relative had died. I even wrote a long essay about it and couldn't understand why other people weren't more affected by the death. My coworkers thought this was a little bizarre to say the least. They were not surprised by my bipolar diagnosis later that year.

In addition to these episodes, I had done some reflection that year about my life and how it was going, as I often do. I went back through the events of the most recent previous year, and decided that every three or four months, I would go through a 'Thing.' (Not to be confused with a Man Thing. Evidently, I am not very creative in my naming!) I even told David about this. I said, "Every three or four months, I am going to go through a Thing. It could be a good Thing, it could be a bad Thing, but there would definitely be a Thing, and whatever it would be, it would be pretty intense."

Surprisingly, even though it seems obvious now, it never, never once occurred to me that what I was describing meant I was bipolar, nor did it occur to me to talk to a doctor until the day came that I was in crisis.

The good news about bipolar illness is that there are many effective medications for treatment these days. Previously, this was not the case. When *An Unquiet Mind* was written, the only available treatment was lithium. Lithium has many side effects, and the author was unable to take it. I am so grateful that is not true now because while I always enjoy the hypomanic episodes, maybe even the manic ones, the price is too high. It means another depression is also likely on the way, probably a really bad one.

While there are very effective medications, sometimes finding the right one is a bitch. Doctors sort of have to feel around with what might work, which drug generally does well for a particular presentation. It's basically like taking spaghetti and throwing it at the wall and seeing what sticks. I've been medicated for twenty years now with varying degrees of success. It isn't an always an easy journey, but I am always conscientious about seeking treatment, and I'm grateful to have it available.

* * *

Sometime after David had gone on his hopefully-happy way, the Universe conspired to send me on a journey that led to what I call my Great Depression, one which resisted all medical intervention. The events that led to this, of course, had to do with a man.

I still had a Man Thing.

By this time, there were a number of things going on with me. I had already lost one marriage, just one more life failure for me. I was extremely heartbroken about what this had done to my kids, that familiar wine-press crushing my chest. I was also completely disillusioned with AA. Hadn't a lot of bad things happened to me? Sobriety was supposed to protect me from that. In my mind, staying sober had promised me that any family I started would be happy, unlike my family of origin. That was the most important thing in the whole world to me, and that was left in shambles with my first divorce.

Also by then, my little nest had disappeared. Diane had moved to North Carolina to be with her adorable surfer boyfriend ten years younger than she. A great story, but I was extremely dependent on her. Diane had lived with me off and on after the divorce. After she left, and she had every right to, I myself moved to a place closer to my job. I ended up hating it there, it was in the country and I was very lonely. Tina and her kids, our makeshift family for a while, had moved, and Tina had also gotten married. Patti and her family moved to a bigger home that was farther away from me. My family continued to be emotionally distant, although my kids did play with their cousins, my sister's kids, when circumstances allowed.

So I had a destroyed marriage and tragically scarred children. All my friends were gone. David was gone. My family was busy with other things. Into this lovely little scene stepped Ken. Although I didn't recognize it at the time, Ken was a narcissist like my mother. It was a match made in Heaven.

Ken and I dated for a while and we had a fabulous time. Ken was short, just the same height as me. He wore his shoulder-length hair in a ponytail and rode a motorcycle. He always smelled like oil from tinkering with that motorcycle. He made a good living as a professional project planner for a utility company.

Like any narcissist, Ken was great at wooing. The problem with a narcissist is that their actions are all smoke and mirrors, but at the time, I didn't know that. Ken would shower me with flowers and buy me expensive presents. He took me to chic restaurants and drove me around in his new Maserati. He was extremely intelligent and very, very funny. Narcissists can be positively charming when they set out to be. They make you feel like the whole world revolves around you with a steady supply of boundless attention and flattery. Life around Ken was fabulously exciting and a whirlwind of heady romance. Ken made me forget about all the pain I had been through, and he made me feel loved. So I began a relationship with him.

There was only one problem. Ken had been going through some of his own things in life and had decided to move to Akron, Ohio. He moved there because he had had a great time when he went to the annual AA Founder's Day celebration. Founder's Day is kind of 'the mecca' of AA, and thousands of people come. Ken loved it. So he moved to Ohio, and we had a long-distance relationship. That is, until I called him one day and another woman answered the phone.

To Ken, this was no big deal. "She doesn't hold a candle to you," he would say. The woman was just convenient and I wasn't, and with his self-view and lack of empathy, he couldn't understand why this would be upsetting to me.

After feeling like I was the center of his world, after all

that romantic attention, I just could not make sense of Ken's involvement with another woman. I tried over and over again to sort through it in conversations with him. These conversations were utterly futile, Ken just didn't get it. Unbeknownst to me, he had a narcissistic blind spot that was beyond my comprehension.

This incident with the other woman was the straw that broke the camel's back for me with all the other weight I had been carrying. Among other things, it played to my most terrible insecurities. There was another woman who was better than me like my sister had always been better. Again, I was not good enough. That was on top of feelings of rejection and all the other losses I was feeling so intensely.

* * *

What happened next defies description. It wasn't the exquisite pain of my youth, nor was it The Place With No Words. It wasn't like any depression I had ever had. In other depressions, half the time I would sleep them away. This time, the pain was constant because I couldn't sleep. There was no relief; there was no escape. I don't know why the doctor didn't give me something to sleep, but he didn't. And I cried.

Worse yet, I couldn't pray. The African Mother God was gone. My father, who I always had felt was watching over me since his death, was gone. There was no rich, imaginative spiritual world, there was only a barren desert. I sincerely would have taken a drink then if I had thought it would make me feel better. I just knew that it wouldn't. I knew I would still be in that barren desert and then I would be drunk and even more miserable on top of it.

My work suffered. Food had no taste, and I lost twenty pounds. Talking to people scared me, I couldn't think of anything to bring up in a conversation. Of course, I wanted another man desperately, and out in the country where we had moved to, there weren't any.

So again, I ended up in a hospital. This time, the doctor I had started seeing recommended it. When my boss heard about the doctor's recommendation, she kindly agreed. "You are not yourself," she said. That was an understatement.

This time, I went to partial hospitalization for three weeks as I still had children to take care of and I could manage that way. I went to the same dirty hospital I had been in when I was first diagnosed as bipolar, but at least I got to go home at night.

At the hospital, I cried. And cried and cried. The staff had groups basically about just changing your attitude. It's based on a book called *Feeling Good: the New Mood Therapy* by David Burns. The staff had good intentions but that was never going to work for me because, looking back now, I know that a large part of what I was going through was grief. Grief for all of it and everyone I had lost. And Grief is a master who cannot be denied.

It was there that I saw the psychiatrist who told me my rhyming during a previous episode had been 'genius.' But he also told me, "Your eyes don't move." Normal people in a conversation will have some animation to their eyes. I didn't. I was virtually catatonic. I was completely dead inside.

It took two years to fully recover from this.

* * *

Ken and I continued to see each other, naturally, what was one to do? There were no other men around, and I needed one. Actually, I think Ken loved it, he loved someone needing him so desperately. A woman needing him so acutely suited him. Ken cultivated vulnerable women he could control. This was a pattern for him. I later came to understand that this is common with many narcissists. Hence, Ken was very supportive during this period even though he was the one who had made the tottering cliff come crashing down around me in the first place.

Eventually, I did the most logical thing. I left my home and my nominal family and my kids (with their father, they were older and more self-sufficient by then), and I moved to Ohio to be with Ken.

* * *

And that was More Mental Illness, and my continuing saga with men.

*A recent picture of Ken with his motorcycle.
I have no pictures of Ken and I together.
I had one good one but I threw it away in a less than spiritual moment.*

CHAPTER 14

Lucy Grealy

Needless to say, the contract I made with Ken, a narcissist, was crazy, and I mean that in a very literal sense. I had to make a contract with him to go out there, he insisted on it, and I had to go out there because of my desperate loneliness. If I moved to Ohio, I had to go where Ken wanted me to go, do what Ken wanted me to do, eat what Ken wanted me to eat, buy what Ken wanted me to buy. I had no freedom or autonomy whatsoever.

The things Ken required of me were not bad in and of themselves. But any agreement like that is bad when your immediate survival and emotional well-being are dependent on doing things to someone else's satisfaction, and when you are always dependent on someone else's approval for everything you do.

Due to my crippled mindset, I did sell my soul and agree to this contract, and I moved to Ohio. This wasn't love. This was need, an imperative. I felt as if I would cease to exist if I continued to be alone, that blankness in my spirit from my youth haunting me.

I was still very ill, but Ohio was very good for me. I liked the AA meetings in Ohio and didn't feel isolated like I had when I lived in the country in Maryland. Ken liked to spend money and we spent a lot of time traveling. We even went to Florida to see his mother. Florida, my favorite place, where I hadn't been in many years. We went camping. We had parties, we had friends, we had fun.

With all the positives, I started to get better. The signs were slow, but I was definitely improving. Even Ken seemed to notice a difference and he started treating me better. We shared many laughs. Ken was the king of practical jokes, like filling the yard with tacky pink flamingoes and then showing up with a new trailer RV. We shared confidences and dreams and myriad intellectual discussions, and we enjoyed our physical and emotional intimacy. Within the confines of Ken's lifestyle rules, which loosened somewhat over time, I was able to be myself, and Ken loved me in whatever degree he could.

Ken and I eventually got married in a small ceremony in our old, solid brick, five-bedroom home with its hardwood floors and the luxury of a built-in library. We had a beautiful candlelit ceremony there surrounded by a few friends. We couldn't get married in a church as no church would have us. Ken had been married too many times before for the church to approve. I was Ken's fifth wife.

Maybe being Wife #5 should have been a clue that I was making a mistake, but I had ways of rationalizing this away. Three of his marriages were when he was still drinking, so those didn't have to count. One was a mistake in sobriety just like I had made with my first husband. Thus I made my status as 'the fifth wife' acceptable in my mind.

Though Ken and I had married, the underlying foundation of our relationship remained fundamentally unsound. There were times Ken would have temper tantrums, like once when I went to the bookstore and stayed longer than he thought I should. He was so furious about me being gone so long that he threw away the book I bought for him.

Ken was often impatient and rude with my children, and he tended to brood if life wasn't unfolding in the household exactly the way he thought it should. I took to sleeping in an extra bedroom on occasion when the strain of Ken's demands got too much for me. Still, I was unable to stand up for myself very well when the circumstances called for it.

Then I became physically ill. It was a strange illness. I was always running a low-grade fever. I had no energy to get out of bed. It was so bad that I had to go on short-term disability from work.

Over a six-month time span, I had many tests done by my primary care doctor. I then went to five different specialists and had more tests. The conclusion at the end of the line was that I was either depressed or suffering from a sleep disorder. I knew I wasn't depressed. I know very well what that feels like. Besides, my symptoms were physical, not mental. I had also already had a sleep study done, so I knew it wasn't that either. The frustration mounted over time with all the doctors. I had reached a dead end, and I was still sick.

Doctors can be infuriating when they discount people. It's very disrespectful in my opinion, yet there was absolutely nothing I could do about it. My frustration became a slow burn in my chest that had no release. Then I lost my temper with my primary care physician, which in this case only cemented his opinion that I wasn't sick, I was crazy.

I had started to see a counselor by then, Dr. Bendo. We talked about what was going on with my illness and talked some about the past. I told the counselor what had happened in Maryland with my Great Depression. I eventually told Dr. Bendo about Ken and the dynamics of our marriage, the first time I had been honest with myself or anyone else in quite a while. I went on to tell Dr. Bendo that I didn't think I could survive one more loss of a loved one. That was the tie that kept me with Ken, that kept me from standing up for myself. It was the fear that I would lose him and that would cause me to go back to The Great Depression I had been in before.

Dr. Bendo was surprised by my assessment. He said, "What do you think is going to happen to you?" But I knew. I knew how far gone I had been before, and there was no reasoning with the fear of repeating it.

Meanwhile, I got more and more frustrated with the internist and other specialist doctors. I finally felt that the only way I could get their attention was to be in a hospital, and the only way I was going to do that was to fake a mental health crisis. Don't get me wrong, I was headed for a manic episode, but I wasn't suicidal, nor was I a threat to anyone.

Having made this decision, I called 911 and told them I was suicidal even though I really wasn't. When the paramedics came, my blood pressure was sky high, and I was still running that mysterious fever. One of the paramedics yelled at me. "How can you consider suicide when you have children to take care of? How can you be so selfish?" I told the other paramedic, "That man needs to get another line of work!" At least my sense of irony was still with me.

After a little while, the paramedics did take me to the hospital in the ambulance. Interestingly enough, while I was in the ER there before I was admitted to the psychiatric ward, both my temperature and blood pressure returned to completely normal. But there I was, in the hospital again. At least this hospital, in downtown Akron, was generally clean and had a large area outside the psychiatric unit where we patients could all congregate and smoke cigarettes.

The psychiatrist at the hospital wasn't a great one, but he did do one thing for me. After fishing around with some questions about my life, he started to see a problem with me. I think he thought I was having a problem with work. He finally said, "There's something in your life you're not dealing with, and until you deal with it, you are going to continue to be physically ill." When the doctor said that, I recognized it was true. I was not dealing with my contract with Ken.

The other thing that happened to me while I was in the hospital was that I read a book. It was called *Autobiography of a Face*. I had heard the author, Lucy Grealy, on NPR a while before that, and then somehow the book fell into my lap, so I read it.

In the book, Lucy relates her story. Lucy described growing up with half a face. She had had a rare form of childhood cancer when she was young and had had a lot of surgeries. The doctors had to remove half the lower side of Lucy's face, and reconstructive surgeries were not successful.

This obviously led to a lot of problems for her. Her family was dysfunctional in the way they dealt with her, although in all fairness, it's a rough situation to deal with. The worst part for her was the way the kids treated her at school. The end result was that she grew up believing no one would ever love her. That the things other people had, like relationships, she would never have.

Sound familiar?

In fact, after reading Lucy's book and relaying the story of my life to a friend, it dawned on me. In my own way, I had had half a face, too.

I finished reading the book while I was in the hospital. By then, I actually was a little bit manic, but I was in a safe place and the doctors got it under control, so it passed without incident.

Unfortunately, the story of Lucy does not have a happy ending. After writing her book, Lucy died of a drug overdose. Which is tragic, but the Afterword written by one of her friends after Lucy had died was what struck me the most. It hit me like a ton of lead bricks.

Lucy's friend, Ann Patchett, another very successful writer, wrote the Afterword. In it, Ann went on and on about how wonderful Lucy was. Ann talked about Lucy's courageous spirit, her spirited politics, her terrible but joyful dancing.

And then Ann said, "What Lucy was not good at was being alone."

Then I saw it. I saw what I could not see before. I saw that I was exactly, exactly like Lucy, and I saw in me all the good things Ann saw in Lucy.

Then somehow, in some way, in some kind of God thing, in another moment of Grace, it finally struck me. All of the sudden, I knew it would be okay to be alone.

After all the years, all the long, long years since I was a child and was somehow lost to myself, I was finally whole.

All I could do was cry tears of joy and relief. It was a similar sense as when I had stood outside myself when I first related the story of my abuse to my first counselor. Then I had seen the child crying who had been a victim. This time, I saw a world where I would be okay with me.

When I got out of the hospital, I left Ken.

If you are like me and struggling with similar things, I can say for a fact that the same is true for you. Try to think of yourself the way people who love you do. They see the very best in you and they are right, though sometimes it is hard to believe. If it feels like there is no one like that in your life right now, pray, and God will send someone to reveal it to you, although I can't say how fast He will do it. He works in His own time, and in His own mysterious way.

***

It may sound like it was an easy, logical decision to leave Ken, but it wasn't. Relationships are complicated, and they change over time. In the three years we had been together, as my had need decreased, my love for Ken had increased. We had so many tender moments over the years, interspersed between the controlling behavior that had gradually subsided to some degree. Ken was a narcissist like my mother, but like my mother, he possessed a haunting, sweet vulnerability that called to me. Generally, behind the smoke and mirrors of a narcissist, there lives a fragile child.

One event in particular stands out. It occurred in the spring before I went to the hospital. By then, I was getting emotionally stronger, strong enough to step away for a minute. I don't know exactly what prompted it, maybe just a general feeling of suffocation, but one weekend, I decided to go away alone. I didn't go far, just to a hotel up the road, where I read poignant books that made me cry and ate lots of chocolate and smoked cigarettes, all no-no's at home. I originally only planned on staying one night, but one turned into two, which turned into three. Then I went home.

I just remember Ken looking utterly forlorn when I got

home. First, he told me I looked 'radiant,' which I supposed I did, I felt so spiritually renewed. Then he hugged me tightly and said, "I don't know what I did that made you leave like that, but I never want to do it again. You're the best thing that ever happened to me." Then together, we cried.

I suppose some psychologist could come up with an unflattering explanation of what was going on, but whatever the reason, Ken and I by then had a bond. I loved Ken, and in his own way, Ken loved me. Your heart calls you in life and there is no denying it. You love who you love, whatever the reason.

Thus started my mission to save my marriage after I left. As with my first marriage, I had the profound sense that a divorce was all so unnecessary given there were two people involved who loved each other. All I wanted was my autonomy, but that autonomy was not intended to be a threat to Ken. If only I could convince him of this! Unfortunately, from what I've read, that is not a concept a narcissist can grasp. Still I kept trying, trying to reconcile, just without the unholy contract we had previously made.

We did go to counseling for a couple of sessions, but evidently, even though I made a long list of things I loved about him, Ken took my request for autonomy as an attack. That's what he told our friends anyway. So divorce proceedings went ahead. Then the divorce proceedings turned into a nightmare I could never have imagined in a million years.

***

When I left Ken, I literally left with nothing but the clothes on my back and a few personal items. At first, I stayed in an Extended Stay facility, hoping the separation would only be temporary. One of the other things that made this difficult is that I had established no friendships of my own. All our friends were mutual, even the ladies. There were three ladies in particular I felt close to, and for their own unrelated reasons, they took Ken's side. Again, I was alone.

One of the ladies involved was a lawyer, and although this was questionable due to our mutual relationships, she represented Ken in the divorce. When the filings for court came through, I was stunned. The filings included seventeen pages of complete lies about me, and my 'friend' had written it. There I was sitting with literally absolutely nothing, and Ken was suing me for tens of thousands of dollars, and my friend was helping him. The sense of betrayal was immense. Eventually, that got sorted out in my favor, but the emotional damage had already been done.

This situation eventually became socially and economically unbearable. My life was getting torn to pieces, and all I could see was the people all around us, close friends but also AA acquaintances, standing by and watching it happen and not caring. Looking back, I don't know what I expected people to do, have some kind of righteous anger for me? There was nothing anyone could do, but that didn't stop me from calling people out on it. You can imagine that this was not a popular strategy. Eventually, the situation between Ken and my friends and the others got so bad that I had to Akron entirely and move to another town not too far away near Cleveland. I had to start over in a place where I knew absolutely no one.

When the day came that I had to move from the Extended Stay facility to my new apartment in my new town, there was one man who agreed to help me. Ken did agree to let me use his truck to move the few things I had left at his house, a wooden rocking chair, an exercise bike, a few other little things. That day brought a flood of tears. I can just remember going to the quick stop at the gas station that I frequented, crying as I asked if they had boxes for moving. I remember going to the post office to change my address with tears streaming down my face. Going to the house and getting my last things where I bent in half over my car in body-wracking sobs, jagged pain lacing through my body. The tears seemed unending. Fortunately for me, God was taking me to a better place, I just didn't know it yet.

* * *

After all this, one would think I would be furious at Ken and glad to be rid of him, anyone with any sense would feel that way.

Surely, if I had any sense, that would have been my approach, but it wasn't. Maybe it would have been if my heart didn't want so badly to still believe in fairytales. My heart has certainly proven to be stubborn! I just kept hearing Ken say he wanted me to never leave, his forlorn statement that whatever he did to cause that, he never wanted to do it again.

The love I felt wasn't the desperate need our relationship started out with. I was still holding on to my desire to have my autonomy and I wouldn't give that up, but still I thought, "If only I could just get through to him and make him feel safe!" I was blind, fueled by a misguided determination that I didn't understand would never bear fruit. I like to look at this in the best light. In this best light, I see this as true unconditional love.

So my efforts continued. At one point. Ken said I could come back if I basically would make another narcissistic contract with him, except this time also give him all my money to control. That was even worse than before! Now that I was better, I wasn't willing to do it.

During this time, Ken's mother died, and this brought us together for a bit. We actually went on a camping trip together and we had a wonderful time. There, Ken basically said that if I agreed that everything that went wrong in our marriage was my fault, we could get back together. I wasn't willing to do that either.

After the camping trip, I came home to my apartment in my new town, Berea, Ohio. There I had another God experience. At that apartment, in that time where I had been able to give unconditional love to someone, my father appeared to me. It wasn't a physical presence, it was just a sense that he was there. What my father was saying was, "You done good. I'm proud of you." I said, "But Dad, what about all the things I've done wrong, what about all the sex things, what about not being monogamous with one person my whole life and all that stuff?" He said, "It's not about that, it's about who you are. It's not about any of that, it's about who you are."

I don't really know if this was my father visiting from

beyond or a Heavenly Father come down to see me. Maybe by this point, these are one and the same, my father joined with the One. I do know that I consider this my third tangible God experience, and as these visits always do, it left me in awe and filled me with an wondrous sense of peace, and this time also bathed in a glow of surrounding Love.

* * *

Ironically, that God experience led me to continue what became an utterly futile year-long crusade. I was a woman on a mission, after all. I did everything in my power to persuade Ken to come back to counseling with me. I always reinforced how much I loved him, that my desire for things to change in some areas was no threat to him.

At one point, I did sue Ken for slander over some things he told people about me that weren't true. At first, I filed this suit because I was angry but then it became something different. It seemed to me a way to have Ken hit a bottom with his emotional issues and face a truth, just like a practicing alcoholic on the verge of recovery. Once Ken did that, he would then come to terms with these issues and get better, and we would then live happily ever after.

Right now, I know that sounds utterly ridiculous, but I really believed it. I saw coincidences everywhere around me, even the littlest things. I considered this serendipity God's way of telling me I was on the right path. I found signs in everything all the time. The fact that God found me a slander lawyer right down the street from where I worked. Every unexpected conversation with Ken, depending on how it went. Every song that came on the radio. I would sit for hours in candlelight listening to meditation tapes feeling like I was pouring my hopes and dreams into the ears of God all the while. Now I call this my "year of magical thinking". Someone wrote a book about that. Different circumstances, but I had that same kind of year.

Nevertheless, despite all my Herculean efforts on my 'mission to save,' after a year, the obvious and inevitable divorce came anyway. When the divorce papers came, all I could do was stare at them for a long time. The loss seemed incredible to me. The voice in my head kept saying over and over, "This is wrong. This is not the way this story is supposed to end."

Yet at age forty-five, there I was, my second marriage finally over. My frog was never destined to become a prince with a kiss.

* * *

The following year was a difficult one for me. I was in pain from the grief, and I blamed Ken for it. I would regularly wander bookstores for hours and hours on end looking for the book that would tell me how to make the pain go away. I never found one, or at least the only one that made sense to me was the one that said, "To make the pain go away, you have to lean into it first." Made sense to me. As was often my habit, I wrote and wrote to deal with my feelings. Although my poetry is not the greatest, that fall, I wrote a poem about it:

Trees in Fall
Will the trees in fall always remind me of you?
And so,
Will the trees in fall always sting me so?
    I loved you.
I loved you when the trees were green and shining, too.
And when the streetlight shone in the bedroom after we made love,
With my arms around you.
But most of all, with the trees in fall.
They're so beautiful.
    So were you.

How harsh it is to have this peaceful beauty taken from me
By the ceaseless bleeding razor pain
    Caused by you.
You didn't have any right to do that to me.

Trees in fall
    And a million other memories.

Ashes and pain
And a million other memories.

During this time, I experienced my second crisis of faith, although this one was not so overwhelming as my first one. I was angry at God for what I saw at the time as God betraying me. I felt all those 'coincidences' had turned out to be God lying to me. This crisis of faith didn't last as long as the first one I had had fortunately, and did not cause the same depth of despair, but it did take quite some time to subside.

In later, better years, when I would relate this story to my friends, I found I could have a little laugh about it. I would look at my friends with a smile and tell them, "When I get to Heaven, God has some 'splaining to do!" I've learned to be a little wary of serendipity and trusting in 'coincidences.' Maybe sometimes, these are just my wishful thinking.

* * *

Fortunately, when I moved to my new town, I did find some really wonderful AA meetings, including a women's AA meeting that I went to for many years. These women gave me the emotional support I needed in what was for me a very challenging time.

One lady in particular befriended me. During this time, she would call me every single day and say, "You won't always feel this way." I didn't really believe her but it was enough to get me out of bed every day. Eventually I woke up one day, and it was true. I didn't feel that way anymore, or ever again. Thank God for friends.

Also when I was new to that group, one of the ladies asked me to do a 'lead,' which basically means that you are a speaker and you share your story. Usually, I don't go into all my problems with men at an AA meeting, but for some reason it seemed appropriate that night. Maybe it was because of what I had been through so recently at the hospital, and/or maybe it was because it was a women's meeting and some women there might relate. I told the stories about both the drinking and the men, I told the story of Lucy Grealy, all of it, right to the very end.

After the lead, it was time for other women to get up and give comments. There were a lot of good comments, but one in particular stood out to me. One lady, Randi, who I knew not at all at the time although I was very, very close friends with her later, stood up and said,

"You had a defining moment."

That was the best way of putting it, and to this day, that is how I describe it.

As for Ken, he later remarried, and he's still married. From what I can tell from sneak peeks on Facebook, Ken and his wife are happy, and I am glad for them.

* * *

And that was Lucy Grealy and my defining moment. But I was only forty-five, and God wasn't finished with me yet. He still isn't.

CHAPTER 15

42 Hamilton St

While I was going through my divorce from Ken, I lived in a two-bedroom apartment with two of my sons. It was a dingy place with no balcony, no patio, and no outside doors. It was time to move. We looked for a house to rent. At first, I never considered buying, but turns out buy I did as circumstances just seemed to click into place to arrange it.

During the time we were waiting to move, I also happened to watch *The Hitchhiker's Guide to the Galaxy*, and that's when I learned about the significance of the number 42. "The answer to life, the universe and everything else." Serendipitously, (apparently true this time!) the house number was 42, and indeed the sign of good things to come.

In The Hamilton House, or '42' as we sometimes called it, everything I had ever hoped for in life came true.

It wasn't a fancy house. It wasn't a big house. It was a small bungalow, modest on the outside with wonderful wood floors and wood trim on the inside. It was bordering on a 'century house,' and it had many stories to tell. At night, I could hear the walls whispering the stories of the people who had lived there before, those experiencing The Roaring 20s or The Great Depression, the Second World War, the happy 50s, the rowdy 60s, or the little girl who grew up there in the 90's who once came to visit me after she was grown up.

There were two particular things of value in living in that house. For one thing, it was surrounded by trees. It was like living in a wonderful woods, cool and serene, softly buffered from the hustle and bustle of the hectic outside world. The house had a delicious smell of damp earth and forest and old oiled wood. It was also close to Cleveland's extensive and magnificent Metroparks, always suited for biking or riding.

When I first moved there and told my mother I was going for a walk in the park, she was gravely concerned. I think she imagined DC parks as highly dangerous. But when she finally came to see me, she fell in love with the parks. My mother also liked my house, and in her typically racist way, she happily judged my neighborhood as "nice, white, middle-class America".

The second wonderful thing about that house was The Sacred Porch. It was where friends and neighbors gathered and shared stories and philosophies and solved world problems reminiscent of something out of *The Divine Secrets of the Ya Ya Sisterhood*. There was only one man who was ever allowed to visit there, and that was the man across the street who had been recently divorced. He got an exception, he later married one of my friends.

And friends I had! Me, the pariah in middle school! Wonderful friends. Talented friends. Mischievous friends. Soulful friends. Funny friends. Loving friends. We had lots of parties at my house. We had parties for Fourth of July, we had parties for New Year's. In the winter, we would have 'Game Nights' and play games by the cozy fireplace. In the summer, we would play badminton. There is only one friend gone from there I truly miss, and that is Randi. Randi was a wicked badminton player if there is such a thing. Speed feathers all the way. I personally couldn't keep up with her!

Randi was a truly inspiring person. She was muscularly built, rode a motorcycle, and had tattoos, a little different from the world I grew up in. But her heart was the biggest, there was room for everybody. I have dedicated this book to her for a specific reason, noted up front. It was our own little joke, the sometimes indistinguishable difference between real honesty and apparent craziness.

Randi and I would go hiking together. We would have long, deeply thoughtful discussions about spirituality and the AA program. Our relationship was deep and rewarding, and it carried us along like a peaceful wide river.

Randi herself was a high school drop-out with many regrets in that regard. When I first met her, Randi was going back to school to take remedial classes in English and Math. She suffered from an inferiority complex. She felt like she was really struggling and was doomed to fail, and often agonized over it. Randi continued to feel that way for the next seven years. But despite that handicap, she valiantly and determinedly persisted, and she finally achieved an amazing result – she got her nursing degree. Tragically, that was her undoing.

After getting her degree, Randi went to work in a hospital. It was grueling work requiring twelve to fourteen hour days, and she was not a spring chicken, she was old like me. I said, "Randi, there are easier nursing jobs, why don't you get one?" Ever determined, ever seeking to make sure she was good enough, Randi said, "I need to make sure I get all my skills right."

Eventually, the pressure got to her and she started shooting up drugs, beginning at the hospital, I believe, where drugs were accessible, and ending with street drugs. The street drugs killed her. She was a true victim of the opioid crisis, just like Lucy Grealy. Randi had been clean and sober for nineteen years before she picked up again. The disease of addiction is exceedingly patient and powerful.

I will never, ever forget Randi. I miss her every day. I think, "If she were here, where would we be walking today? If she were here, what would we be talking about?" I think of her fierceness. She was fierce in the way she lived, in the way she worked, in the way she loved her friends, in the way she loved her family. But the 'not being good enough' killed her anyway.

Feeling like you are not good enough can kill you. Two

things – if this is you, one, do the things that need to be done to get over this. Start being honest. Take responsibility for your life. Let go of the past.

The second thing is for the rest of us, and it comes from an old James Taylor song. It's the one thing we can do to maybe help keep our loved ones alive.

"Shower the people you love with love."

Then, hopefully, they will know they are good enough.

* * *

Besides my friends in the neighborhood, other friends of mine came to visit Hamilton House from out of state. Patti came to see me several times. She and I went and stayed on Lake Erie a couple of times, a wonderful place. We went to the Butterfly House in Put-in-Bay on South Bass Island every time Patti visited. Butterflies are always a beautiful metaphor for our transformation.

Patti and I also had a lifelong learning experience on one of her visits. This had to do with growing plants. In my new house, for my beautiful porch, I had purchased begonias. I bought begonias because they didn't need a lot of light, and the porch was a bit obscuring. I had other potted plants outside around the house as well. They were all dying and I couldn't understand why. Patti came out and she, in her no-nonsense teacher way, instructed me, "They only need Miracle Grow once a week." I had been giving it to them daily. When the plants started dying, I thought it was because they needed more water when really they were already drowning. I was killing them with care. This taught me a big lesson about killing with care, which I also applied to overparenting my sometimes-troubled children, a crime I am frequently guilty of.

But in that place and time, I said to myself, "That's enough of that," and I had some beautiful custom-made hanging flower plants crafted for me, and I hung them from my porch overhang. Everyone complimented me on them, so I guess they achieved their goal. They made everyone's day a little brighter. That's a good goal for a plant, even a not-really-alive one.

Today, I am trying the plant thing again. I have some real

plants, and as long as I get them out of the rain when it is raining too much, they do wonderfully. I also bought a gardenia, to remind me of Florida. Not sure the gardenia is very happy here, but we are giving it a try, and I've had 3 blooms so far, so that's a success story for me!

* * *

The only thing that was 'missing' from Hamilton House was a man, and for the first time in my life, I didn't mind it. My Man Thing had drifted entirely away at long last.

I can remember hearing so many times in my life that you need to love yourself before someone will show up, but once you're okay with you, God will send you a man. Once you're okay with yourself, and with being alone, some nice, healthy man will just show up when you least expect it, magically, but only when you are not looking for it.

I'm here to tell you that's bullshit. I know this because I was okay at Hamilton House being by myself, in fact, I was reveling in it, yet no man magically appeared. I always thought that was silly anyway. If your ulterior motive for getting good at being alone is really to get a man, that's an oxymoron.

But Hamilton House did prove the Lucy Grealy case. I had finally, finally, finally gotten good at being alone, and so I didn't need a man to be really happy. My defining moment held true.

If you are like me, and you have a Man Thing, I can only tell you that the best thing you can do is to live your life honestly. Love honestly, with all your heart. Take the pain when it comes to you, even and especially the pain that comes when you have to walk away due to the unhealthiness of the relationship. And do that. Walk away if need be, even if you love him (or her as the case may be) with all your heart.

If you do these things, sooner or later, healing will come to pass. That is what will show up when you least expect it. Then you will have your own defining moment. I do not promise you a man, but I do promise you will be happy. Within the confines of life's ordinary ups and downs at least.

* * *

As I write this, I realize some of the most meaningful things that happened to me in that house happened from a distance, and these had to do with my mother.

My mother had mellowed as the years went by. Not sure why, maybe age did it. Maybe her old fears were not so paralyzing. I also once read that the best way to get along with a narcissist is to put some distance between you. Apparently, that helped in my case, at least. I was in Ohio, and Mom was in Maryland. That greatly improved my standing. Additionally, when I was having such difficulty with my mental illness episodes, I think she had decided that my feeling better was more important than anything else. Whatever the reason, I am thankful for it.

One story means the most to me. After my mother was in an assisted living facility, I went to visit her. She was moving things around and organizing them as she always had since I was a small child. She had something in her hand, and she looked at me and said, "I have something I want to give you. This came from your Dad. This was the first thing he ever gave me, and that's when I knew I was going to marry him. This was the first thing he gave me, and you were the last thing he gave me, so I want you to have it." (My younger brother, I suppose, being a different kind of gift because he was adopted.)

In any event, it was a touching story, but I knew my mother had a vivid imagination and a poor grasp of reality sometimes, so in my mind, I kind of poo-pooed it until one day when I was looking at her beautiful wedding picture, and I realized she was wearing it. It is a distinctive cross, very original. It's gold, with a miniature rosary strung around it, right down to another tiny cross at the end of it. You can't miss it. There it was, in my mother's wedding picture. In the end, my mother saw me as her last important gift from my father, not as The Second Child.

* * *

I do know now that despite all my terrible childhood years, all my mother ever really wanted was for her children to be happy. When I was growing up, maybe she was so demanding because she had real fears about us getting into Heaven. Yes, being a narcissist made her unbearably exacting, but in her own way, she did love us. When I was younger, we even had a song we sang in one of my mother's rare moments of sanity:

> *"I love you, a bushel and a peck*
> *A bushel and a peck and the heck I do*
> *I love you, a bushel and a peck*
> *You bet your pretty neck I do."*

I always loved it when my mother sang that.

Later, when all of us kids were all older and my brothers and I each had spells of financial difficulty, my mother would help us. I remember one time my brother needed something, and my mother was agonizing because at that moment, she wasn't able to take money out of her investments right away to help him, though eventually she did. My mother did her best to help all of us.

So surprisingly, nay, astonishingly, in the end, all my mother really wanted, for all of us, was what every mother wants: her children to be happy.

All in all, my mother and I had seventeen good years by the time she died, and I am grateful for it.

* * *

And that was 42 Hamilton St., the Answer to Life, the Universe and Everything Else.

The House at 42 Hamilton St

Randi, the face of the opioid crisis

Patti and I at 42 Hamilton St

Diane, the Wise One, in North Carolina

Betsy and I at 42 Hamilton St

My favorite picture of my mother when she got older

CHAPTER 16

Such Is Family

True to form, my mother worked until she was eighty-five. She taught for many years, and then in the course of her required continuing education after my father died, she decided to get her PhD. For several years, schooling was her focus. She received her PhD when she was sixty-nine and went on to become a counselor until she retired. She had shrunk by then due to a deteriorating spine, but while she wasn't the tall mother I remember, she still carried herself very regally. Her face had aged well without many lines, and her hair eventually turned an attractive pure white.

After my mother retired, she devoted her time to the family. On holidays, there she would be, cooking for days. She was in her glory, savoring her progeny all gathered together. But when she was ninety-three and I was fifty-three, my mother became very ill and probably would have passed away. I was ready for this. However, Betsy wasn't, so she and her children went to extraordinary lengths to save my mother, even giving her pep talks about how many parties she would be going to.

While she went to a few, my mother never went to many parties after that. She became incontinent, ended up in a wheelchair, and at times, was intractable. She spent the last years of her life in an 8 x 10 room in a nursing home with some of the family pictures and paintings on her walls, the only touches of home. She had a painting of my father on the walls, and as she got senile, she amusingly said, "I had a lot of husbands, but your father was my favorite one." The nursing home smelled like the nuns who ran it, slightly stale, and bathed in the vapor of institutional food.

Later I blamed Betsy for the years my mother spent in the nursing home. What about how she had lived her life made Betsy think my mother would have wanted to live that way? My mother had temper tantrums there, and it was no wonder given the circumstances. All because Betsy had not been ready to let my mother go.

At least my mother was entertaining in her old age, and very appreciative. I would drive down from Ohio to see her, and she would tell me invented stories about how she grew up on a horse farm. One day, she went on and on about one of my uncle's paintings hanging on her wall. There was a mountain by a lake in the painting. She then told a fantastical tale about how that mountain had erupted like a volcano, and how she had gotten a boat and saved her mother from it.

Often, my mother would wax on and on about how lucky she was to have had such a loving family. In her eyes at that time in her life, everyone in the family had always been happy, and everyone in the family had always loved each other. When she had her hip surgery at Christmas one year, the hospital was empty, so my sister and I, with our children, were allowed to follow as my mother was wheeled to the pre-operating room. On the way there, my mother exclaimed, "This is the meaning of rich!"

On the other hand, sometimes she didn't recognize me. This was unpredictable. One day, she would be in her fondly reminiscent mood, then the very next day when I went to see her, she didn't know me. Once, when I reminded her I was her daughter, my mother said, "I don't have any daughters."

For some reason, this never bothered me. This harkened back to the day when my first counselor told me, "Some days, you are going to go over there and your mother is going to spit in your face and slam the door. You just have to turn around and go back on a better day." This life lesson had stayed with me for all my adult years, and that's what I did.

It was in her more difficult times that my mother would have her temper tantrums. Later the staff realized that rather than using mood medication as was sometimes given to geriatric patients, all it took was a cookie and her temper tantrum would go away. In that way, she became very childlike at the end of her life, which always made me feel very tender.

My mother's stay in the nursing home still causes some ambivalence for me. While I wish my mother had not had to spend her last years like that, for my sake, I am glad to have had her.

***

My mother passed of old age very peaceably when she was ninety-eight, although it wasn't so peaceable between me and my siblings. Betsy and I had been taking turns staying with my mother. My brothers couldn't face seeing my mother like that, so we didn't see them.

Like my father at his death, by then, my mother had stopped saying much. In fact, she didn't say anything at all when I first got down there to see her. She just lay serenely, her white hair framing her elderly face, and only once looked up and said, "I love you." This was particularly touching as I had never heard her say this in my entire adult life.

Betsy, as was her way, did not want my mother to go. Hence, when my mother stopped eating as the elderly often do when they are ready to go, she insisted that the staff at the nursing home keep feeding my mother, even against her will. This was agonizing for me. On one of the last days, I was at the nursing home alone with my mother. While I was there, the nurse's aide came in to feed her, and she was getting very upset about it. At one point, she loudly yelled, "Go away!" This is the last thing I ever heard my mother say.

Betsy and I were texting back and forth by then, so I

texted her about this. She completely ignored me. At the very same time, exactly simultaneously, she was texting the rest of the family on another group text, including my siblings and all of our children. Betsy informed the rest of the family that my mother was still eating. My younger brother, Chris, said, "Thank God for that."

Thank God for that? How could he possibly say that? How could he not know how wrong this was? So even though I knew it would make me a family pariah once again, I proceeded to let my family know my thoughts. Chris blasted me. He was so rude about it that my oldest son had to step in and tell my brother to stop disrespecting me in front of the whole family. But my sister stopped forcing my mother to eat.

Three days later, my mother passed. When she passed, my sister was in the room saying the rosary, just like my mother had done for my father as he lay dying. Then, in one quiet moment, my serenely sleeping mother simply stopped breathing. I was ready for this. It was long past time.

* * *

I don't know why I got the mental illness and alcoholism and Betsy didn't, although if you remove all the trappings, my sister suffers from something, too. Being The Firstborn Child didn't work out too well for her. Growing up, she was so symbiotic with my mother that she never developed the internal compass we all need to navigate life. She just always did what my mother told her to do, and she always thought what my mother told her to think.

In adulthood, Betsy and my mother had moved in together, Betsy's family of six and my mother. Actually, they built a house together in Davidsonville, Maryland, that my mother designed, and my mother had an apartment in it. The Davidsonville house was a McMansion that had the luxury of two baby grand pianos. My favorite room was the sunroom overflowing with my mother's plants, the smell of delicious, sweet blooms from her snake plants suffusing the air. The sunroom was framed in my mother's habitual custom floor length drapes. Many of the beloved things I grew up with moved there, including my father's oak desk and my mother's gold-etched china.

When my mother and sister built that house, my sister was forty. For whatever reason, at that point, my sister began to see the mother the rest of us always knew. This recognition was difficult for Betsy, it rewrote her whole reality. She then went on a mission to figure out what was wrong with my mother, and why. When she talked to Tony about it, he just said, "Betsy, how could you not know? Mom's always been like this."

By this time, Betsy was forty-five. Imagine being forty-five, and suddenly realizing everything you based your life on, from beginning to end, was built on an overwhelming fracture. This was the very same fracture that had birthed all the fault lines in my family, my mother and her own secrets, whatever they were, mental illness included. Betsy came to me then and apologized for always supporting my mother when I was in trouble. Finally, Betsy understood what I had been rebelling against. But one has to have a compass, right? So for Betsy, this became extreme, fanatical Catholicism, and getting more family educational degrees. Turns out my sister is crazy, but in very socially acceptable ways.

Just like my mother.

In a way, Betsy has become like the protagonist in my Uncle Erv's story, HEMEAC, trying to survive based on a somewhat-outdated system of perfection and rules, and I am the 'savage' outside. But my God isn't her God. Though He may be only a minor God, He is a God just the same. My God only values gritty honesty, and He does not suffer fools. He has had other names, and other forms and other incarnations in my life, but right now, I call Him 'The God Who Is On My Side.' That's as opposed to 'The God Who Lets Bad Things Happen to Me.' I don't pray to that God, it's an exercise in futility.

Still, in the end, it turns out no one is 'better than.' Not Betsy with her highly successful doctor and CPA children, or me with mine, carrying the family curse. We are just the same, both people trying to do the best we can with the hands we were dealt. She's not responsible for much of her life and her children's lives, nor am I responsible for much of my children's and mine. That was capricious genetics, maybe capricious gods, and probably some PTSD.

Betsy will, of course, find a way to discount this story, and I will have to find a way not to buy in. But it's hard not to buy in when you're outnumbered in a family, and when you are the family scapegoat. It is the system I started with, after all, and those children, my siblings, are the ones that I loved.

* * *

Betsy and I are estranged for a variety of reasons. Most recently when her daughter got married, she did not invite my children to her daughter's wedding. First cousins. After all the years, all the holidays, and the relationships our children had built, my children were not good enough to go.

My brother Tony had a rather sad life. His first marriage failed when his wife was caught cheating with his best friend. He lived with another woman for a while who got pregnant and had a baby. Tony was terribly attached to that baby, and even took care of the baby after the mother had left both of them. Later, Tony found out the child wasn't his, and the mother came and took the baby away, that baby he loved. And that was the end of that. Since then, Tony has worked hard, he always did. He's never remarried nor had any other girlfriend that I've known. He has come to family dinners, and in his gruff, sardonic way, still loved us. Now he's disowned me, because of my politics.

Sadly, my younger brother, Chris, passed away while I was writing this book. When I had earlier gotten news that my brother was sick, I really didn't know how I felt. At that time, Tony had advised me to call Chris but I never did, I'm not sure why. Maybe it sounds selfish, but all I could think about was how Chris had subtly treated me poorly for many, many years, all the way back to my early years in high school. How when he got remarried, I found out on Facebook. How much it hurt when my mother was dying and he called me selfish because I insisted that they stop force-feeding my mother as she lay on her deathbed.

Yet it seemed to me there was no cataclysmic rift to be healed that one could point to, no opportunity for some dramatic moment of reconciliation to be had when he was nearing the end. There has to be some kind of closeness to have an identifiable rift, something has to be there first for it to feel torn apart, so it seemed there was nothing to say. As it was, I said my goodbyes in my head.

Just days ago, as I sat here writing, I received the news, fittingly via Facebook, that Chris had, in fact, passed away. Despite the distance inherent in our relationship, I was sad when I got this news. He was my brother, after all. At one point in time, we were part of the same family, we were part of the same story. We came from the same place ever so long ago. This is a circumstance that can never be erased.

Oddly, as I was writing and pondering Chris's death, I had the sense that as his spirit started its journey to be with the Powers-That-Be, Chris came to sit with me awhile. The sensation was palpable. It was as if he were passing through me, and I felt he was telling me, "Regina, I love you, I've always loved you, and I'm proud of you for writing the book. It's a story that needs to be told." Maybe in death, he's the brother I always wished he would be, and now, maybe I can be the sister I always wanted to be, at least in my heart.

To some, this may not seem like a happy ending to this story, and yes, in many ways it is quite tragic. But this story was never about happy endings. It was about forgiveness; forgiveness of me, for being The Second Child and not being good at it. For not being as good as Betsy, for not giving my children the life I wanted them to have. And only now, even as I write this, I realize it's also to acknowledge that I stole that second place away from its rightful owner, my brother, Tony. And in my crazy family, I did want to steal it.

* * *

As you age, there inevitably comes a day in your life when you realize that all the things from your childhood, all the things that once defined you, are gone. Today I found out that the father of the neighbors, the ones across the street where I often took haven when I was a child, is passing. Almost every one of that generation, the generation before me, is gone.

Recently, I received word through other family members that Betsy sold the house in Davidsonville that she and her family had shared with my mother. Now all the familiar things of my childhood are gone, all the last vestiges: the pianos, my father's desk, my mother's china just when I am at the age when I am rediscovering their importance.

It's odd, the things you remember. For whatever bizarre reason, lately one memory stands out for me vividly, and that was when our family would get ready for parties. Although it always meant work for me, preparing for a family dinner party always felt right. I knew what was expected of me. The table had to be set just right. The house had to undergo a thorough cleaning, more so even than usual. Even as I write, I can feel myself dusting the bookshelf with its familiar worn books that I had read many times.

As I dusted the bookshelf, I felt cocooned in an aura of anticipation. I knew that when the company would come, my father would be in his element, and my mother would be in hers. And I would feel safe.

Other valued memories play around the edges of my mind as well - a young me dancing around in the living room while Betsy played the piano. Tony making jokes at the dinner table. Chris and I lighting charcoal snakes while we waited for evening on the Fourth of July. The three younger of us giddily sliding down the laundry chute when we were still small enough. My brothers and I excitedly climbing out onto our tiered flat roof to play, on the rare occasion Mom let us. All the memories of my father.

A childhood is many things.

Remembering my childhood brings to mind my father's mother, Grandma Nona, when she went into a nursing home near the end of her life. I remember all the grown-ups tsk-tsking and cluck-clucking because all Grandma Nona would talk about was her childhood. The conclusion was that my grandmother had gotten senile, that she was losing her wits, but as I look at this now, I understand how my grandmother felt.

Of all the times in my life, I miss my childhood the most.

Surprising, isn't it? For all the problems, those were the times that formed me. Everything else after that was just a trapping I accumulated as I got older. This even includes my children, who are on their own journeys.

I'm glad, at least, that at this point in my life, I remember my childhood years so fondly. I can put myself right there in my mind, dusting that bookshelf, feeling that cocoon of anticipation.

I embrace the richness of the memories.

Despite our current circumstances, I will always love my sister and my brothers, even such as we are, adrift on an ever-changing sea. We will be forever tied, bound by the steady, unchanging, and powerful currents, the ones that have always flowed beneath us.

Such is family.

EPILOGUE

As might be expected, the abuse I suffered as a child still affects me in small ways, little anxieties that rear up here and there, The Rules echoing in my head. But the abuse does not define me. Nor does my alcoholism or my mental illness. I am a human being, with all the richness and complexity that entails. I am not a pathology.

Instead, I can say that my life experiences have transformed me. Transformation is a marvelous curative. It took me from being a pariah-with-cat-glasses to being 'brilliantly sassy', cat glasses and all. The exact same photograph of a ten-year-old me with an entirely different view. Transformation also took me from seeing myself as The Second Child to seeing myself as the last important gift my father gave to my mother. I look at myself differently. As Diane would say, "We can never be rid of the emotional scars of our childhood, but we can step into our spiritual selves and be whole."

On a more practical note, I am beyond grateful to still be sober after thirty-five years given all life has seen fit to send me. As for my mental illness, I have pills I take in the morning, and pills I take at night which right now, at least, are effectively keeping me stable. Some pills with food, some on an empty stomach. None of the medication is addictive. It's a bitch to manage it but manage it I do. My mother would say I am fat, an infraction against the pretty Rule, but it's due to the medication, and it's a small price to pay.

I continue to go to AA meetings and, having had fourteen years of therapy in early sobriety, I now occasionally stop back in for a tune-up. I still enjoy my dear, dear friends. Most importantly, The God Who Is On My Side occasionally stops in for a visit. It's clear to me now, and yes, it is a cliché - everything in my life was always leading to this moment, even the many countless desperate times I couldn't see it. You have to trust the process even when it is hard to, though I admit that more times than not, I couldn't do it.

* * *

During the first year of my Great Depression, the year I was literally virtually catatonic, my therapist gave me a book. It was called *From Misery to Meaning in Mid-life*. Not sure I remember much of it, but I do remember two things. One thing the author observed is that we don't tell high-school children the truth. As the graduates sit there in their caps and gowns on their auspicious graduation days, we give them inspiring speeches, and we lie to them. We tell them that life will be their oyster and great things lie ahead for them when really, a lot of very difficult challenges lie ahead for them. Maybe that isn't true for everyone, but it was certainly true for me.

The second thing is that there is only one way to get meaning out of life, and that is to serve. I think I've tried to do that in my sobriety when life allowed me the time and resources to do it. To me this has been my lifeline, my purpose-driven life. "Our primary purpose is to stay sober, and help other alcoholics to achieve sobriety." Maybe this book is a way of serving, too. Maybe this book will actually get published, and maybe it will actually help someone, although frankly, I'd consider that a grand freak accident, or maybe Divine intervention, were it to come true.

I also read another book once called *If You Want to Write* recommended by my dear friend, Diane. The book isn't just about writing, the subtitle describes it as *A Book about Art, Independence and Spirituality*. About writing, the author said, "Everyone is talented, original, and has something important to say." As for women, she wrote a chapter called *Why women should neg-*

lect their housework to write, and that's when I knew that book was for me. After all, I had a bumper sticker on my car when my kids were young that said, "My only domestic quality is that I live in a house."

The author, Brenda Euland, contends that the meaning of life is to create. She bases that on artists like William Blake and Vincent Van Gogh. She describes them as so joyful in the way they created, and claims this joy comes directly from God, from Divine inspiration. William Blake once said, "Imagination is the Divine Body in every man," and I believe it. I even had that quote across the top of the wall of my classroom during my brief stint at teaching.

At this point in my life, I can only agree with both authors. There are only two purposes in life that give us meaning, and those are to create and to serve. Hopefully, I do both. I know that when I do, I feel at peace.

* * *

In my life, Gods come and Gods go. It's not that they are different Gods, they are just the forms I need at the time, the forms that I can understand at any given moment. I can't understand Infinity, I can only understand small parts of it at any given time, so that's how this goes. There was the African Mother God after my divorce from Big Dave, the Jesus I met when I was seeing David in jail, the Father who visited me after my divorce from Ken who took the form of my Earth Father, and the God whom I happen to have now, The God Who Is On My Side. Even the God Who Lets Bad Things Happen to Me. And don't confuse things. The God Who Lets Bad Things Happen To Me is not a bad God, he's certainly not the Devil, although I don't like Him very much. Often, I feel like I'm angry at Him and He is the only one I see. Those are the times I've suffered a crisis of faith.

But we need what some people might call the 'bad' God. I never understood why, and certainly in the bad times, I wouldn't go along with this, at least I wouldn't like it. But in the good times, I am aware of it. I came to realize this most when I lived at the house on Hamilton Street. Life was really good there. I was having so much fun that I was feeling joyful. So much fun that I forgot the pain. In that state of mind, the Joy at times became something almost frivolous. Like a helium balloon without a tether that just drifts mindlessly away. Then I realized, the pain is the tether. It is what grounds us, it is what gives the Joy meaning. Without pain, Joy is nothing. Thus we have the God Who Lets Bad Things Happen to us, who really also loves us, too. I am thankful for all the Gods who have given me the life I've had. I know that for all the tears I have cried, and there have been many, I have also laughed just as many laughs.

Find your God; it will help you. It doesn't matter if it is a He, She, or It. It doesn't matter if He, She or It is white, black, red or even alien. How do you find a God, you ask? You just imagine one. What would you like your God to be like? God can be anything because He is Infinite. Imagine the kindest person you ever met. Or pray to a loved one who has passed on, like I did with my father. Or borrow one of my Gods. Or try organized religion if that works for you, hopefully one without too much dogma.

Be patient with yourself, and with God, if you can't see One in times of trouble. Although God may not seem to be there, and I of all people understand that feeling, I promise One is.

Find your God.

* * *

I don't go to church. It's not that there's anything wrong with going to church. It's right for some people, it just isn't for me. One would suppose that's because of my history, although I always did like the music and the sanctuary.

I also don't know what Heaven is like, but my father was very dramatic about it. Frequently he would go on about it, the same story every time. "Regina," he would say. "Do you know what Heaven is like?" I would dutifully say no, though I had heard this lecture many times before. "In Heaven, you have a Glorified Body, and you will live for Infinity. Do you know what Infinity means, Regina?" I would say no, though I had heard this lecture many times before. "Infinity means that when you get to Heaven, you can spend as much time you want with everyone you want to, and when you are done, you get to start all over again!" This was apparently an amazing idea to him, there were so many people he would want to meet.

Then he would say, "Do you know what St. Paul said about Heaven, Regina?" And again I would say no, though I had heard this part many times before also. My father would bellow loudly, "St. Paul said, 'Eye has not seen, and ear has not heard, NOR HAS IT EVEN ENTERED THE MIND OF MAN TO CONCEIVE of all the Wonders that await us in Heaven!'" My father would always yell that part. I always thought he was impressed by that because he knew he was a genius, and he thought that if it was something that even he couldn't conceive of, then it must be unimaginably wonderful.

Diane had some other theories about it; we talked about it many times. She would say everyone goes to Heaven. Earlier on, I would say, "Some people don't. Child abusers don't. People who torture people don't." I wasn't really thinking of my own experience, I just thought people who deliberately hurt people shouldn't get to go. Later on, I came to a different conclusion. I said, "God will let everyone in, but there are some people who don't want to go so they go to Hell, which is a separation from God." Diane would say, "But if they choose not to go, it's because something is broken, and God will fix it. So those people go to Heaven, too."

These conversations would always remind me of a song my father used to sing at Easter. At my father's funeral, the choir director called it "that Protestant piano-banging song," and he wouldn't have it. It's a beautiful song called *The Holy City*. It starts with a haunting, yet reverent, story about a dream of a Cross on a hill in Jerusalem. Jerusalem is then razed to the ground, but the Savior comes, and Jerusalem is triumphantly restored to glory. I always had a favorite part of the song, though my feelings about this were sometimes mixed up with The Rules and my secrets and my many venial sins. The song went like this:

> *" The light of God was on its streets*
> *The gates were open wide*
> *And all who would might enter*
> *And no one was denied…*

"All who would might enter, and no one was denied." All would enter. Catholics or non-Catholics, sinner or saint. All would be in Heaven in the end.

* * *

I don't know what the afterlife is like. Diane has theories about this, too. "Maybe there's a Heaven where souls go to live. Maybe there's reincarnation. Or maybe there is just a stream of light that our souls will stream into, a smaller part of a bigger whole." Which would mean we would be connected to everyone and everything, which sounds really nice, but on the other hand, we might lose our identities, too.

Frankly, I'm afraid to die sometimes, not knowing what it will be like. I only hope that on my deathbed, I will understand it better, and I won't be afraid to go. Hopefully that won't be that far away, relatively speaking, because I don't think I want to live to be ninety-eight like my mother. But who knows, by the time I get there, maybe medicine will be so advanced that I will. In that regard, only time will tell.

* * *

My children and I dance a delicate dance. The journey goes on, ebbing and flowing with the individual circumstances each son faces. I don't have any grandchildren yet, and perhaps I never will. We have a family joke that maybe the gene pool will be better off for that. But while not all of my children are exactly where I want them to be, and while sometimes their situations are challenging for me, I have to trust they are exactly where they are supposed to be. Trust the process. After all, look how long it took God to get me straightened out. Only most days, I wish God would be in a bigger hurry with them. It would certainly make life easier for me.

***

I'm still not good with men. Likely just as well, because for the last sixteen years, neither of the Gods, for good or for ill, has seen fit to send me one. Today, I find this mostly amusing as 'I am enough', all alone though I may be. It only serves to remind me of one thing, if one (not me) believes in the theory that being okay alone is what makes a man show up.

The Gods have a weird sense of irony.

***

In the real world, in the outside world, I'm lucky to have a good job, just like normal people. I work in the computer science industry at a bank where I've been for over eighteen years. Over time, the workplace has shifted from office to home, affording me many opportunities, the most important one, in this case, being that I can work wherever I am. I literally can be anywhere I want to be. And there's no one left to please. So I have decided. I am moving to Florida.

To be in Florida, where I was always happy.

ACKNOWLEDGEMENT

Many thanks to the ladies who have walked this journey hand in hand with me, Diane Gregory, Patti Todaro, Lida Widdersheim, and my cousin Katherine Niederhelman, aka Laffy Kathy. I dare not even try to imagine where I would be without you.

Much gratitude goes out to Alexander Watkins, whose encouragement and enthusiasm as I have been writing this book have been invaluable.

Thanks also goes out to Lee Ann Finlay, my roommate from college, who has always supported my writing and was an early reader of this book. Her support has been very welcome.

Finally, I thank my children, Dominic, David and Patrick, who have supported me while I was writing this book. They have provided me with many good suggestions which no doubt improved this book. For this and many other things, I am indebted to them.

.

Made in the USA
Las Vegas, NV
22 August 2021